Introduction to
Results-Oriented Management and Accountability (ROMA) for the Community Action Network

Frederick Richmond
The Center for Applied Management Practices, Inc.

Barbara Mooney
National Peer-to-Peer ROMA Training and Certification Project

Version 5.1 – 2020

Published by The Center for Applied Management Practices, Inc.

Copies may be ordered from:
The Center for Applied Management Practices, Inc.
320 Lamp Post Lane, Camp Hill, PA 17011
(717) 730-3705; www.appliedmgt.com

IMPORTANT DISCLAIMER: This publication is intended to provide general information and should not be construed as legal advice or opinions concerning any specific facts or circumstances. Consult an experienced attorney if advice is required concerning any specific situation or legal matter. Neither the author nor the publisher make any warranties, expressed, or implied, with respect to the information in this publication. The author and publisher shall not be liable for any incidental or consequences damages in connection with, or arising out of, the use of this book.

Contact the authors in care of The Center for Applied Management Practices, Inc., or by email at:

info@appliedmgt.com

Printed in the United States of America

ISBN: 9780-9787249-8-6

Introduction to Results-Oriented Management and Accountability for Community Action Agencies and CSBG Eligible Entities

5.1 Participant Manual
March 2020

"Introduction to ROMA" was originally created from material developed by Frederick Richmond, President, The Center for Applied Management Practices, Inc. (CAMP) in the early 1990s. In 1998, Richmond's work became a part of a Train-the-Trainer project known as the "Virtual Outcomes College," under the direction of John Wilson, Executive Director of the Community Action Association of Pennsylvania (CAAP).

Since 2004, this manual has been a collaboration between Richmond and Dr. Barbara Mooney, Director of the National Peer-to-Peer ROMA Training and Certification Project.

The material has been modified over the years based on the authors' observations of practices in the Community Service Block Grant (CSBG) network and on changes in policies at the federal level. Changes have also been made as a result of feedback and input from numerous National Certified ROMA Trainers and Implementers across the country. Thanks to everyone who has made a suggestion for improvement! Special thanks to Terry Bearden, Carey Gibson and Joanne McClain who helped us get this manuscript ready for printing.

For more information, see the following web sites:

www.appliedmgt.com
The Center for Applied Management Practices, Inc.

www.roma-nptp.org
National Peer-to-Peer ROMA Training and Certification Project

www.ANCRT.org
Association of Nationally Certified ROMA Trainers and Implementers

Foundational Principles
Building on the Work of Peter F. Drucker and Reginald K. Carter

In *Introduction to Results-Oriented Management and Accountability (ROMA),* we use two management methodologies to support the principles and practices for implementation of ROMA: *Five Most Important Questions* from the Peter Drucker Foundation and the Seven Key Questions from Reginald Carter's, *The Accountable Agency.* The use of the Drucker and Carter questions in this manual demonstrates their alignment with ROMA.

Peter Drucker, sometimes referred to as the world's greatest management thinker of all time, provides us with a series of questions to assist in considering the overall management of the agency. The Carter material extends the framework by providing us with accountability questions.

Drucker's management theory as we know it today began a century ago. It was intended for government and nonprofit institutions at the turn of the century, most notably in 1901 for the U. S Army and later in 1912 for the nonprofit Mayo Clinic. It found its way into the for-profit sector in the 1930s during the Great Depression. *The Five Most Important Questions* clearly support the principles of the ROMA Cycle. They can be considered to be the basic "ABCs" of the language of performance management.

The Seven Key Questions were first published by Sage Publications in 1983 in *The Accountable Agency,* by Reginald K. Carter. Together with Harry Hatry of the Urban Institute in Washington D.C., Carter developed what became known as Client Outcome Monitoring, one of the predecessors of ROMA. When Carter developed the seven questions, he prefaced them with the following paragraph, "Each year when a program manager presents a request for funds, there are seven key questions that legislators, funding agencies, and top administrators should ask:" These questions are as relevant today as they were when originally written, and versions of the questions are now found throughout many other management systems. They are at the core of agency and program accountability that is essential to the ROMA Cycle.

There are many performance management and continuous improvement systems used by both for-profit and non-profit entities. ROMA is the system based on federal legislation and guidance related to the Community Action primary funding source: the Community Service Block Grant (CSBG). It is the performance management system adopted by representatives of all levels of the CSBG network over the past 30 years.

Table of Contents

Ten Questions

Please circle either "True" or "False" for each of the questions below.

1. True or False: "ROMA" is the term for the required reporting of data to state and federal government funding sources.

2. True or False: Each phase of the ROMA cycle is unique and is most effective when conducted in isolation from other phases.

3. True or False: The ROMA Cycle is completed when reports are compiled and submitted.

4. True or False: Community Action agencies (CAAs) most effectively evaluate their results by focusing on the activities supported exclusively by the Community Services Block Grant (CSBG) which sponsors ROMA.

5. True or False: The 2017 National Theory of Change maintains the historic National Goals, including family, agency and community goals, but is in graphic form.

6. True or False: The focus on results instead of the provision of services will reduce the agency's competitiveness and marketability because of low numbers of results reported.

7. True or False: "Outcomes" and "Services" are different terms for the same concept.

8. True or False: According to the Organizational Standards, when creating the agency plan, CAAs are required to select services they will offer based on funding they have available.

9. True or False: Implementing ROMA in your CAA will affect the planning and fiscal functions, but will not affect the way programs and services are delivered.

10. True or False: ROMA Next Generation is an improved management system because it uses different foundational principles than the original ROMA created in 1994.

Module One

History, Purpose, and Perspective

Key Points – Module One:

- Results-Oriented Management and Accountability (ROMA), as a set of principles and practices, has grown out of a rich history – the understanding of which can help us identify future actions.
- The National Theory of Change includes the core principles of the CSBG network and the focus on achievement of results.

History, Purpose, and Perspective

1964 – The Beginning

Congress passed the **Economic Opportunity Act**, establishing and funding Community Action Agencies and Programs.

1970 – The Mission and the Model

The issuance of **OEO Instruction 6320-1** established the mission and the model (family, agency, and community) of Community Action:

"To stimulate a better focusing of all available local, state, private, and Federal resources upon the goal of enabling *low-income families,* and *low-income individuals* of all ages in rural and urban areas, to attain the skills, knowledge, and motivations and secure the opportunities needed for them to *become self-sufficient."* Family

"The Act thus gives the CAA a primarily catalytic mission: to make the *entire community* more responsive to the needs and interests of the poor by *mobilizing resources* and bringing about greater institutional sensitivity. A CAA's *effectiveness,* therefore, *is measured* not only by the services which it directly provides but, more importantly, *by the improvements and changes it achieves in the community's attitudes and practices toward the poor and in the allocation and focusing of public and private resources for antipoverty purposes."* Community

"In developing its strategy and plans, *the CAA shall take into account the area of greatest community need, the availability of resources,* and its own strengths and limitations. *It should establish realistic, attainable objectives, consistent with the basic mission established in this Instruction, and expressed in concrete terms which permit the measurement of results.* Given the size of the poverty problem and its own limited resources, the CAA should concentrate its efforts on one or two major objectives where it can have the greatest impact." Agency

Note: This instruction memo was signed by Donald Rumsfeld, then Director of the Office of Economic Opportunity.

1974 – What's in a Name? The Community Services Act

The **Economic Opportunity Act** was terminated in 1973, and replaced with the **Community Services Act of 1974**. At this time there was no longer a cabinet level presence to administer the act, but there was still a direct relationship between the federal office and local CAAs.

The change in name may have given an erroneous signal to those in the field who did not study the funding legislation -- to make a change from providing opportunities to delivering services. However, while the name of the legislation was changed, **the mission and purpose of the funding remained unchanged.**

1981 – The Block Grant A Change of Relationship

The Community Services Act was replaced by the **Community Services Block Grant (CSBG) Act of 1981.** This changed the regulatory and funding basis of Community Action Agencies and the relationship between local agencies and the federal government.

State offices were now installed as recipients of the Block Grant funding and, therefore, as intermediaries for local Community Action Agencies. States were given responsibilities for submitting "community action plans" to identify how funding would be distributed to local agencies, and for assuring that the local agencies were meeting identified community anti-poverty needs.

While the relationship changed with this legislation, **the mission and purpose of the legislation did not change**.

1993 – Measurement and Accountability GPRA

Congress passed the **Government Performance and Results Act (GPRA)** in response to a renewed emphasis on accountability.

> "The purposes of this Act are to – improve Federal program effectiveness and public accountability by promoting a new focus on results, service quality, and customer satisfaction … and to help Federal managers improve service delivery, by requiring that they plan for meeting program objectives and by providing them with information about program results and service quality."

These points were made regarding the expectations of the Act:

- Establish performance goals to define the level of performance to be achieved by a program activity.
- Express such goals in an objective, quantifiable, and measurable form.
- Describe the operational processes, skills, technology, and the human capital, information, or other resources required to meet the performance goals.
- Establish performance indicators to be used in measuring or assessing the relevant outputs, service levels, and outcomes of each program activity.
- Provide a basis for comparing the actual program results with the established performance goals.
- Describe the means to be used to verify and validate measured values.

1994 – Six National Goals

The 1994 Amendment to the CSBG Act, in response to GPRA, specifically mentioned a requirement for CSBG eligible entities to provide outcome measures to monitor success in three areas: promoting self-sufficiency, family stability, and community revitalization.

In August of 1994, Don Sykes, then director of the Office of Community Services (OCS), created the Monitoring and Assessment Task Force (MATF). The MATF was established to increase the focus of the CSBG Network on performance and results issues as they relate to the work of assisting low-income people. The MATF produced several products, including a National Strategic Plan and the Six National Goals **for community action that specifically addressed the three areas** identified in the 1994 amendment**, and added agency goals.**

Goal 1. Low-income people become more self-sufficient.
(Family)

Goal 2. The conditions in which low-income people live are improved.
(Community)

Goal 3. Low-income people own a stake in their community.
(Community)

Goal 4. Partnerships among supporters and providers of services to low-income people are achieved.
(Agency)

Goal 5. Agencies increase their capacity to achieve results.
(Agency)

Goal 6. Low-income people, especially vulnerable populations, achieve their potential by strengthening family and other supportive systems.
(Family)

1994 – Introduction of ROMA

The Monitoring and Assessment Task Force (MATF) advised the Office of Community Services (OCS) to support the development of its own management and accountability practices.

The MATF recommended a system to be known as "Results-Oriented Management and Accountability," or ROMA.

ROMA was defined as "a performance-based initiative designed to preserve the anti-poverty focus of community action and to promote greater effectiveness among state and local agencies receiving Community Services Block Grant (CSBG) funds."

Beginning in 1994, ROMA provided a "framework for continuous growth and improvement among more than 1,000 local community action agencies and a basis for state leadership and assistance toward those ends." OCS provided a number of tools and training programs to help individuals in the network increase their understanding of ROMA.

At this time, ROMA implementation was voluntary.

In his 1994 "Testimony on Reauthorization of the Community Block Grant Program," Don Sykes, then Director of the Office of Community Services (OCS) identified the ROMA approach as a way "to help agencies identify cost effective strategies for reducing gaps in services, improve the capacity of CAAs to partner with innovative community and neighborhood-based initiatives, and help communities better understand the agency's goals and achievements. Timetables for experiencing success from ROMA, which is voluntary, will vary from community to community."

1996 – ROMA Applied in the Network

According to OCS guidance from 1996, "ROMA is a framework for marrying traditional management functions with the new focus on accountability. It is the common language for CAAs to use to respond to the Government Performance and Results Act of 1993, which requires that federally funded programs demonstrate measurable outcomes."

ROMA incorporates the use of outcomes/results into the administration, management, operation, and evaluation of human services.

Local CAAs were asked to focus on the achievement of outcomes in addition to the traditional counting of customers and units of service.

The ROMA "Train-the-Trainer" program, created in 1997 by the Community Action Association of Pennsylvania and The Center for Applied Management Practices, was first funded by the Pennsylvania Department of Community Affairs, which was responsible for administering CSBG funds in the state. Starting in 2000, to stimulate the implementation of ROMA across the country, OCS continued the development of a series of tools and practices to increase standard understanding of underlying principles and concepts and to help local agencies embrace ROMA through a network of National Peer-to-Peer (NPtP) Certified ROMA Trainers.

Sample Family Level Logic Model created for the NPtP Project*:

Organization: Program: □ Family □ Agency □ Community

Problem Statement	Service or Activity	Outcome	Outcome Indicator	Actual Results	Measurement Tool	Data Source	Frequency of Data Collection and Reporting
(1) Planning	(2) Intervention	(3) Benefit	(4) Performance	(5) Performance	(6) Accountability	(7) Accountability	(8) Accountability
Organization or Program Mission:							

**F. Richmond modified the Logic Model created by Joseph Wholey to meet the needs of the CSBG network.*

1998 – Reauthorization of the CSBG Act

Congress enacted the 1998 Reauthorization of the CSBG Act that included language to **mandate implementation of a comprehensive performance-based management system** across the entire Community Services Network. **ROMA was identified as this system.**

The 1998 Reauthorization required outcome reporting from all CAAs and CSBG eligible entities beginning October 1, 2001.

2001 – Direction from OCS for the First Mandatory Report

The Office of Community Services issued **Information Memo (IM) 49** – Program Challenges, Responsibilities and Strategies – FY 2001-2003.

In this IM, State Offices and CSBG Eligible Entities were provided with guidance regarding the implementation of ROMA and core activities to assist them in preparing for mandatory performance reporting.

In addition to identifying Core Activities required of both state recipients of the Block Grant and local Eligible Entities that ultimately receive the funding, Margaret Washnitzer, then Director of the Division of State Assistance in OCS, asserted in IM 49:

"The Six National ROMA Goals reflect a number of important concepts that transcend CSBG as a stand-alone program. The goals convey the unique strengths that the broader concept of Community Action brings to the Nation's anti-poverty efforts."

2001 – Direction from OCS for the First Mandatory Report -Continued

Washnitzer further identified important elements of results focused management and ROMA implementation:

Focusing our efforts on client, community, and organizational change, not particular programs or services. As such, the goals provide a basis for results-oriented (not process-based or program-specific) plans, activities, and reports.

- CAAs must not focus on program-based delivery systems, but rather see how programs work together within the agency to promote changes – not just to provide units of service.
- The effectiveness of CAAs is measured by the positive impact on the client, resulting from participation in one or multiple programs of the CAA.
- CAAs work to improve their community as well as their own agency management processes.

Understanding the interdependence of clients, communities, and programs.
The goals recognize that client improvements aggregate to, and reinforce, community improvements, and that strong and well-administered programs underpin both.

- Emphasizes the interdependence of the family, agency, and community levels, whose effectiveness depends on sound agency management.

Recognizing that CSBG does not succeed as an individual program. The goals presume that Community Action is most successful when activities supported by a number of funding sources are organized around client and community outcomes, both within an agency and with other service providers.

- Establishes that CAAs work best in partnership with other community based organizations, that CSBG funds are used to leverage other resources, and that all activities and outcomes of a CAA whether funded by CSBG or other sources are reportable.

Quotes on this page are from IM 49

2005 – Implementation of National Indicators of Community Action Performance

The National Association of State Community Service Programs (NASCSP) had administrative responsibility for the national data collection effort from 1987 to 2018.

To comply with mandatory reporting of outcomes, beginning in 2001, several states created standardized indicators, based on their own aggregation and analysis of the measures that had been independently developed at the local agency level.

Notable among these were the reporting systems established in New York, Missouri, and Minnesota, and the Pennsylvania Family Agency Community System (FACS), which was adopted by several other states and agencies.

These state identified indicators were reviewed by NASCSP, which conducted a comprehensive analysis of the "literally thousands of different outcomes" submitted by states between 2001 and 2003. The 2004 NASCSP report, stated: "To enable greater aggregation and national reporting of the most universal and significant CSBG results among states and local agencies, twelve common categories, or indicators of community action performance, have been identified from Fiscal Year 2001-2003 data."

OCS reviewed the recommendations of NASCSP and established National Indicators of Community Action Performance (also known as the "National Performance Indicators" or NPIs) in May of 2004.

The **mandatory performance reports** to OCS included National Performance Indicator data as of Fiscal Year 2005.

These were arranged by the Six National Goals until 2017 when the NPIs were revised and rearranged for the OMB cleared CSBG Annual Report.

2006 – The ROMA Cycle

As a way to make the directives in IM 49 easier to understand, Mooney and Jakopic* developed the ROMA Cycle graphic seen below. It incorporates the Core Activities for Eligible Entities that are outlined in that directive.

The Results Oriented Management and Accountability Cycle

Assessment
Community needs and resources, agency data

Evaluation
Analyze data, compare with benchmarks

Planning
Use agency mission statement and assessment data to identify results and strategies

Achievement of Results
Observe and report progress

Implementation
Services and strategies produce results

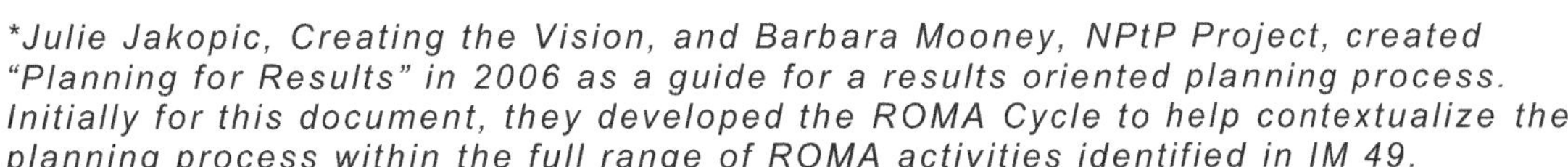

**Julie Jakopic, Creating the Vision, and Barbara Mooney, NPtP Project, created "Planning for Results" in 2006 as a guide for a results oriented planning process. Initially for this document, they developed the ROMA Cycle to help contextualize the planning process within the full range of ROMA activities identified in IM 49.*

2009 – The Obama Administration Focus on Results

In January 2009, OMB issued the Performance Progress Reporting Form *(PPR)* -- a standard, government-wide performance progress reporting format which is used to collect performance information from recipients of federal funds. The ROMA Logic Model was included as PPR Appendix C.

Other key elements of the administration's focus include:

- Emphasis on place-based services to address the causes and impacts of poverty;
- Increased accountability for performance;
- Promotion of evidence-based practices to achieve results.

2010 – GPRA Modernization Act

Action was taken to modernize the federal government's performance management framework, retaining and amplifying some aspects of the Government Performance and Results Act (GRPA) of 1993, while also addressing some of its weaknesses.

GPRA 1993 established strategic planning, performance planning and performance reporting as a framework for agencies to communicate progress in achieving their missions. The GPRA Modernization Act established some important changes to existing requirements.

The intention of the law was to change behaviors in the executive branch by creating a more explicit fact-based decision-making framework to implement programs and be more results-oriented. They understood that, for the law to be effective, the principles included had to be embraced beyond the executive branch – <u>by all entities that receive federal funding.</u>

2011 – A New Strategy for Excellence

Stimulated by GPRA Modernization, the Office of Community Services began directing a strategy to improve performance of the CSBG network. Funding was provided to support a new approach to streamlining the CSBG T/TA resources*. The plan was to encourage interoperability among the various resources.

OCS developed a national plan that included the following four priority areas:

1. **Performance Management and Data** – OCS will work with national technical assistance partners and State CSBG lead agencies to **build upon the performance management structure developed through the Results Oriented Management and Accountability (ROMA) system** and the current National Performance Indicators (NPIs) that are used to assess program performance.
2. Governance and Legal Technical Assistance.
3. Risk Mitigation and Quality Assurance.
4. Centers of Excellence.

** From IM 123, Reorganization of CSBG T/TA Resources*

2012 – Focus on Performance Management

The Administration for Children and Families (ACF) Office of Community Services (OCS) began a process to improve the support of high quality services delivery across the CSBG network. As part of a broader effort to increase accountability and achieve results, OCS launched several initiatives: to establish organizational standards for eligible entities; to enhance the CSBG Network's performance and outcomes measurement system for local eligible entities (ROMA); and to create state and federal level accountability measures to track and measure organizational performance by State CSBG Lead Agencies and OCS.

2015 – Several Performance Management Improvements

– Organizational Standards

The purpose of the organizational standards is to ensure that all eligible entities have appropriate organizational capacity, not only in the critical financial and administrative areas important to all nonprofit and public human service agencies, but also in areas of unique importance for CSBG-funded eligible entities.

– State and Federal Accountability Measures

The State and Federal Accountability Measures are designed to track organizational performance by State CSBG Lead Agencies and OCS. These measures are part of an enhanced framework for accountability and performance management across the CSBG Network.

– Automated State Plans

The new Model State Plan streamlines and automates the prior Model State Plan content while also incorporating information on the Organizational Standards and State Accountability Measures.

– American Customer Satisfaction Index (ASCI)

Use of the ACSI will allow OCS to collect consistent, uniform information from eligible entities across the country, and will provide the states with actionable insights to improve their customer experience and boost program results. This is in keeping with the enhanced emphasis on using data for analysis and decision-making to continually make program improvements.

Additional efforts to modernize the overall performance management approach continued for several years.

2017 – New Annual Report

The new CSBG Annual Report* marks the largest overhaul of CSBG data collection and reporting since the first comprehensive CSBG Information Survey (CSBG-IS) was developed in 1983. OCS and the CSBG Network – composed of CSBG Eligible Entities, State CSBG Lead Agencies, State Community Action Associations, national partners, and others – have participated in a multi-year effort to update the CSBG Annual Report that was designed to complement ROMA Next Generation and support and complete the CSBG Performance Management Framework. The information in the new CSBG Annual Report will be used at local, state, and national levels to improve performance, track results from year to year and assure accountability for critical activities and outcomes at each level of the CSBG network.

*Excerpt from IM 152- 1/19/17

The new CSBG Annual Report (AR), approved by the Office of Management and Budget (OMB) on 1/12/17, includes:

- Connection with the Automated State Plans
- Identification of State Accountability Measures
- Reports on American Customer Satisfaction Index
- Reports on Organizational Standards for Local CAAs
- New National Performance Indicators for Communities, Families and Individuals
- Identification of Services for Families and Individuals and Strategies for Communities
- Report on Interaction of State and local Eligible Entities regarding performance of full ROMA Cycle
- Inclusion of a National Theory of Change for Community Action

ROMA Next Generation

What has been called "ROMA Next Generation" is a way of talking about an increased focus on the elements of ROMA in the context of the OCS Performance Management Framework. It is also about using some new tools to assure the network is implementing the full ROMA Cycle to achieve results for individuals, families and communities. It relies on the foundational principles of ROMA identified in this introduction and adds:

- Network-wide adoption of a National Community Action Theory of Change.
- Support for creation by Community Action Agencies of local theories of change to improve strategic planning and implementation of services/strategies that will produce outcomes.
- Renewal of the CSBG network's commitment to working toward community change, as well as individual and family outcomes.
- Focus on improved use of data.
  - Increased facility with the collection, analysis and use of data at every point of the full ROMA Cycle.
- Integration of all of the phases of the ROMA Cycle for continuous improvement.
  - Increased connection of identified needs, populations served, services and strategies implemented, and documentation of outcomes using standard indicators of performance.
- Integration of all aspects of the Performance Management Framework (Automated State Plan, Organizational Standards, State and Federal Accountability Measures, ASCI, Annual Report with new National Performance Indicators, and the Congressional Report).

Additional training modules on these and other topics related to the Performance Management Framework will be available through our national partners.

CSBG Performance Management Framework

In summary, the elements of the CSBG Performance Management Framework (PMF) include the following:

- Local Organizational Standards
- State and Federal Accountability Measures
- Results-Oriented Management and Accountability (ROMA)
- CSBG State Plan (automated)
- CSBG Annual Report
- American Customer Satisfaction Index (ACSI) Survey

National Theory of Change

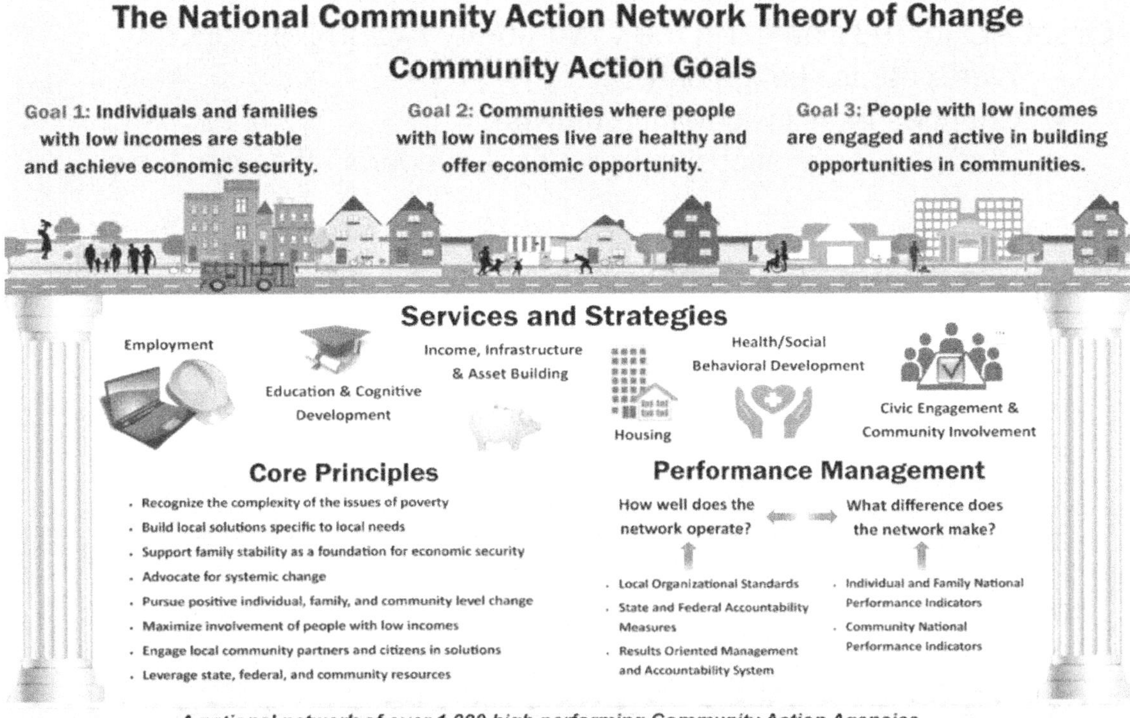

A national network of over 1,000 high performing Community Action Agencies, State Associations, State offices, and Federal partners supported by the Community Services Block Grant (CSBG) to mobilize communities to fight poverty.

This publication was created by NASCSP in the performance of the U.S. Department of Health and Human Services, Administration for Children and Families, Office of Community Services, Grant Number 90ET0451.

Module One Review

Select the best answer for each question or statement. There may be more than one correct answer.

1. The original OEO instructions (1970) included a focus on which level/s of work?
   - Family
   - Agency
   - Community

2. What change did the passing of the Community Service Act in 1974 have on the Community Action Network?
   - Was a name change only
   - Changed the mission of the network
   - Changed the relationship between the federal office and local CAAs

3. What change did the passing of the Community Service Block Grant Act in 1981 have on the Community Action Network?
   - Was a name change only
   - Changed the mission of the network
   - Changed the relationship between the federal office and local CAAs

4. What role did the passing of Government Performance and Results Act (GPRA) in 1994 have on the Community Action Network?
   - Community Action Agencies were asked to increase focus on performance/results.
   - All recipients of federal funds were asked to increase focus on performance/results.
   - No change as the network was already focused on results.

5. The intention behind the Monitoring and Assessment Task Force (MATF) recommendation of the system to be known as "Results-Oriented Management and Accountability" was to:
   - Create a Community Action specific performance-based initiative;
   - Preserve the anti-poverty focus of community action;
   - Promote greater effectiveness among state and local agencies;
   - Provide a framework for continuous growth.

6. The reauthorization of the CSBG Act in 1998 accomplished:
   - Changed ROMA from a voluntary process to one that was identified in the Act;
   - Established mandatory reporting on outcomes and performance;
   - Changed the mission of the network;
   - Changed the relationship between the federal office and local CAAs.

7. What was the role of the establishment of the Six National Goals in 1998?
   - Provided a framework for understanding of the role of the CAA network.
   - Reinforced the concept that CAAs work on three levels (family, agency, community).
   - Was used to help understand the way local CAAs fit into the national network.

8. What was the role of the National Performance Indicators introduced in 2001 and made mandatory in 2004?
   - Provided a framework for standardized reporting among all CAAs.
   - Established that these were the only outcomes that are expected to be produced by CAAs.

9. The GPRA Modernization Act of 2010
   - Prompted the CSBG network to review its practices related to Performance Management.
   - Had no impact because Community Action Agencies are not included in GPRA oversight.

10. ROMA Next Generation means:
   - The basic principles of ROMA have been changed.
   - The basic principles remain with additional focus on some areas.

Module Two – Building Blocks

Part One

The Agency's Mission and Theory of Change

Part Two

Community Assessment

Module Two – Building Blocks

Part One

The Agency's Mission and Theory of Change

Key Points -- Module Two, Part One

- The mission statement, while being short and sharply focused, identifies why the agency is in business and includes key elements of population, service/strategy, outcome, and relationships.
- There is a difference between mission change and mission drift.
- Periodic review will assure that the mission remains relevant, especially if the agency/community experiences change.
- The agency's mission is reflected in a Local Theory of Change, which identifies how the whole agency comes together to produce outcomes.
- A strong mission statement and clearly stated Local Theory of Change communicate an agency's conceptual framework and its approach to addressing poverty.

The Agency's Mission

In Module One, you learned that the original mission of Community Action included:

- assisting families and individuals to become self-sufficient,
- mobilizing public and private resources, and
- bringing about greater institutional sensitivity to poverty.

Peter Drucker, an acknowledged expert in the management field, has identified Five Most Important Questions for agencies to answer. His **Question One, "What is Our Mission?"** gives us this information:

> "Each social sector institution exists **to make a distinctive difference** in the lives of individuals and in society. Making this difference is the mission – the organization's purpose and very reason for being....but *changing lives* is always the starting point and ending point. A mission **cannot be impersonal**, it has to have deep meaning, be something you believe in – something you know is right...."

Drucker further tells us:

> "Defining the nonprofit mission is difficult, painful, and risky. But it alone enables you to set goals and objectives and go to work. Unless the mission is explicitly expressed, clearly understood and supported by every member of the agency, the enterprise is at the mercy of events. Decision makers throughout will decide and act on the basis of different, incompatible and conflicting ideas. They will pull in opposing directions without even being aware of their divergence and your performance is what suffers."

The source of the quote is, The Five Most Important Questions Self-Assessment Tool Participant Workbook, Peter F. Drucker, Third Edition, 2010.

Understanding Mission Statements

Can the organization's mission be communicated clearly and concisely in a matter of seconds?
The effective mission statement is short and sharply focused.

Can the organization's mission be understood by the general public… or your neighbor?
Think of it as a "sound bite."
It should be able to fit on a T-shirt or on the back of a business card.

The four key elements of a mission statement are identified below with examples for each. *You may think of other examples for the elements.*

- Population – Low-income, poverty, special needs, unemployed.
  - Is the population to be served identified? Does the mission identify low-income or other designation? Is there a geographic target for population?
- Services – Social, human, educational, health, community services.
  - Can you tell from the mission statement the types of services that are administered by the organization (or referrals)? As Drucker says "The hospital isn't going to sell shoes and it's not going into education. It's going to take care of the sick."
- Outcomes – Self-sufficiency, independence, stability, well-being, ready-to-learn.
  - Are the expected and achieved outcomes clearly stated? Can you tell what will change?
- Relationship – Partnership, collaboration, referral, agreement, contract.
  - Is there any identification of relationships with other organizations that show the connections that help further the mission?

Activity – Reviewing Mission Statements

<u>Instructions:</u> You have been provided sample mission statements from actual Community Action Agencies, State Community Action Associations, and State CSBG Administrative Offices.

Please evaluate to determine if any, some, or all of the elements of a good mission statement (identified on the previous page) are present. If you find missing elements, consider how adding them would strengthen the sample statements.

Use this page to make notes for discussion with the group.

The Mission as Foundation

The mission is found at the bottom of the logic model, representing the foundation on which the organization is built.

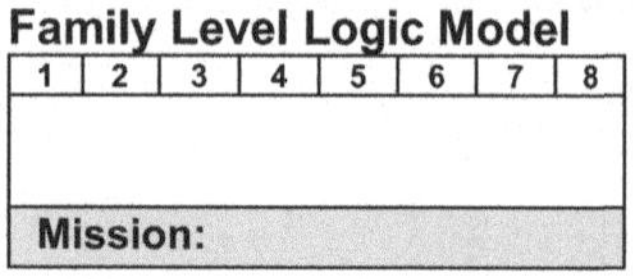

Family Level Logic Model

1	2	3	4	5	6	7	8
Mission:							

Activity – Assumptions Behind Mission Statements

Another way to think about mission statements is:

What does the mission statement say about the agency's **assumptions about poverty** and **its role in reduction of poverty?**

The agency mission statement will tell the public what **change** it expects to make or accomplish. It will also provide some insights into the underlying beliefs and values of the agency board and staff.

Consider: Where does the agency believe its interaction must occur?

- *At the level of stabilizing families (addressing or preventing crisis) before they help them move to self-sufficiency?*
- *At the individual/family level by providing opportunities to develop skills and resources for economic security?*
- *At the community level to address the causes of poverty?*

What Is Behind the Mission?

Instructions: Using the same sample mission statements, consider what someone who hears this could think about poverty, the population in poverty, and the agency's role in addressing poverty.

Use this area to make notes for discussion with the group.

Activity – Writing Mission Statements

<u>Instructions:</u> Practice evaluating the mission statement for your agency or writing one for your specific program.

Don't forget the key elements: Look for references to the <u>population</u> being served, the <u>services</u> they receive, the <u>relationship</u> to the community, and the expected <u>outcomes</u>.

Mission Change or Mission Drift
Sometimes Things Change

The mission statement of the agency or program should be reviewed on a regular basis, for instance as annual strategic planning is being done.

Anytime there are significant changes — which could be economic, demographic, or environmental (natural or man-made disasters) — or when there are changes in the availability of resources, the mission should be reevaluated.

If the agency had a specific objective and it was accomplished, the agency's mission should also be reevaluated.

Caution: You should not change your agency's mission statement without cause. Remember the mission of the Community Action Network, as guided by legislation, has not changed since its inception in 1964. While some language has been adapted, the anti-poverty purpose has been reviewed and found to contain a strong message that is as applicable today as it was then.

Consider the difference between proactively changing a mission statement and passively allowing the agency to "drift" from its original purpose.

Mission Change

Mission Change occurs when the organization:

- has done a comprehensive study of current circumstances,
- has identified a need for restatement of the mission or reorientation of the agency to meet new challenges and opportunities, and
- makes a conscious decision to change the agency focus.

To illustrate when it would be appropriate to change a mission statement, let's look at two examples of organizations that have made specific and deliberate changes to their mission statements.

March of Dimes

This is an example of a mission changed because the organization achieved its goal.

The original mission of the March of Dimes was "To eradicate polio."

What Happened? – They succeeded!

The March of Dimes reinvented itself and today its mission is, "Prematurity is the #1 killer of babies in the United States. We are working to change that and help more moms have full-term pregnancies and healthy babies. From polio to prematurity the March of Dimes has focused on researching the problems that threaten our children and finding ways to prevent them."

YWCA

This is an example of a mission changed because the organization expanded its interests to include new elements.

The original mission of the YWCA was "To provide housing, recreation, and a faith-based community center for young women."

What happened? – The organization changed its focus with a new mission statement: "YWCA is dedicated to eliminating racism, empowering women and promoting peace, justice, freedom and dignity for all."

Mission Drift

Mission Drift is the phenomenon which occurs when an agency departs from its original purpose and core values to take on a task that is perhaps related, but not directly in support of the mission. In some instances, this is a response to external events, such as available funding for something the organization never did before. In other cases, internal events can lead to mission drift, such as major turnover of staff and or board members.

Drucker cautions us to "never subordinate mission in order to get money."

Sometimes taking new money requires so much additional work, or so much attention to new objectives/new populations/new situations, that the new money actually produces a drain on the agency's other programs.

We find Mission Drift when the agency is attempting to add activities without putting them in context of existing activities. This causes a dilution of organizational energies, which are then spread over more functions than can adequately be served.

Drucker advises: "When in doubt whether to head off into another direction because a donor suggests it or a foundation grant opens up a new avenue, analyzing the new direction/activities in relationship to the mission statement will help you stay on course."

Remember that the mission is the basis on which every decision in the agency is to be made.

"The ultimate test is not the beauty of the mission statement. The ultimate test is your performance."

Creating Local Theories of Change

What Does the Agency Expect to Change?

Consider the National Theory of Change (Module One) which is a graphic representation of what the Community Action Network expects to change (the Three National Goals), and what services/strategies will get there.

- A Theory of Change (TOC) is a conceptual road map for how an organization expects to achieve its intended impact.
- While similar to a logic model (which has detailed information about needs, activities, inputs, outputs, indicators and outcomes), a Theory of Change demonstrates the "big picture" about how all of these components work together.

Here is a definition of a Theory of Change:

"A Theory of Change articulates the assumptions about the processes through which intended changes will occur and the organizational capacities to manage such processes.

It specifies the ways in which short-term outcomes drive to intermediate outcomes and how intermediate outcomes create the conditions that make long-term outcomes likely.

It is the bridge that links an organization's concrete, daily operations with its mission."

David Hunter, Theory of Change Glossary, CRE and Hunter Consulting, LLC

Consider the connection between the National Theory of Change and the CSBG mission and purpose as stated in the enacting legislation (Module One). Does the National Theory of Change demonstrate the mission of the CSBG network?

How does the National Theory of Change relate to your agency mission?

Applying the National Theory of Change to Your Agency

Not all local CAAs are the same.

- Each CAA will use the Performance Management Framework in ways that match their identification of local community needs and resources.
- At the local level you will want to demonstrate:
  - How well does the AGENCY operate?
  - What difference does the AGENCY make?

Start by assessing how your agency identifies outcomes.

Does the agency collect data regarding "Program Outcomes" identified in silos?

Or, does the agency coordinate services and strategies to meet overall agency-wide outcomes at all three levels (Family, Agency, Community)?

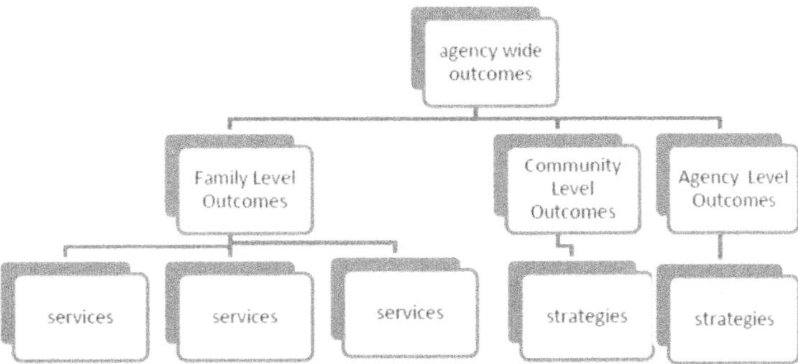

Trying Something New

Think about how "we have always done" the work of the agency.

- What is real, what is true, what is good, what has been done?
- What outcomes (changes) have you achieved in the past?

Think about WHAT ELSE your agency could achieve if you were not focused on the provision of services (but rather on change).

The ideas that are generated by this kind of thinking will influence your creation of your Local Theory of Change.

One agency in Kern County, California, put it this way: What will move our customers out of poverty?

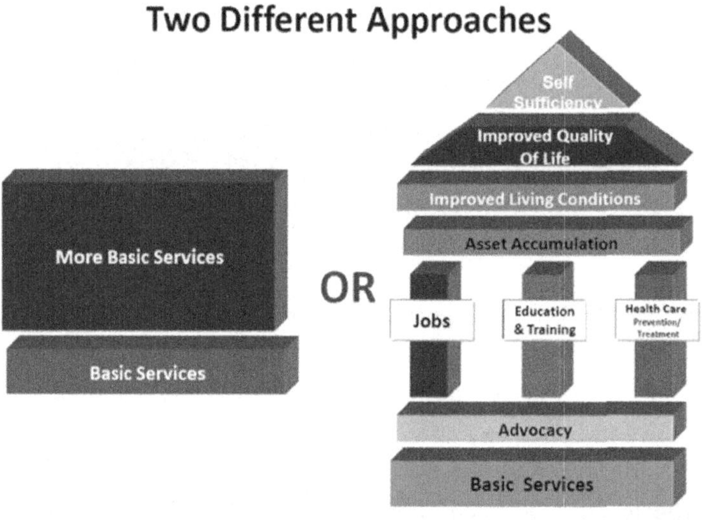

Graphic from Community Action Partnership of Kern County, California

There is considerable assistance available for agencies that want to consider creating a Local Theory of Change. A template that can be used for brainstorming is found on the next page.

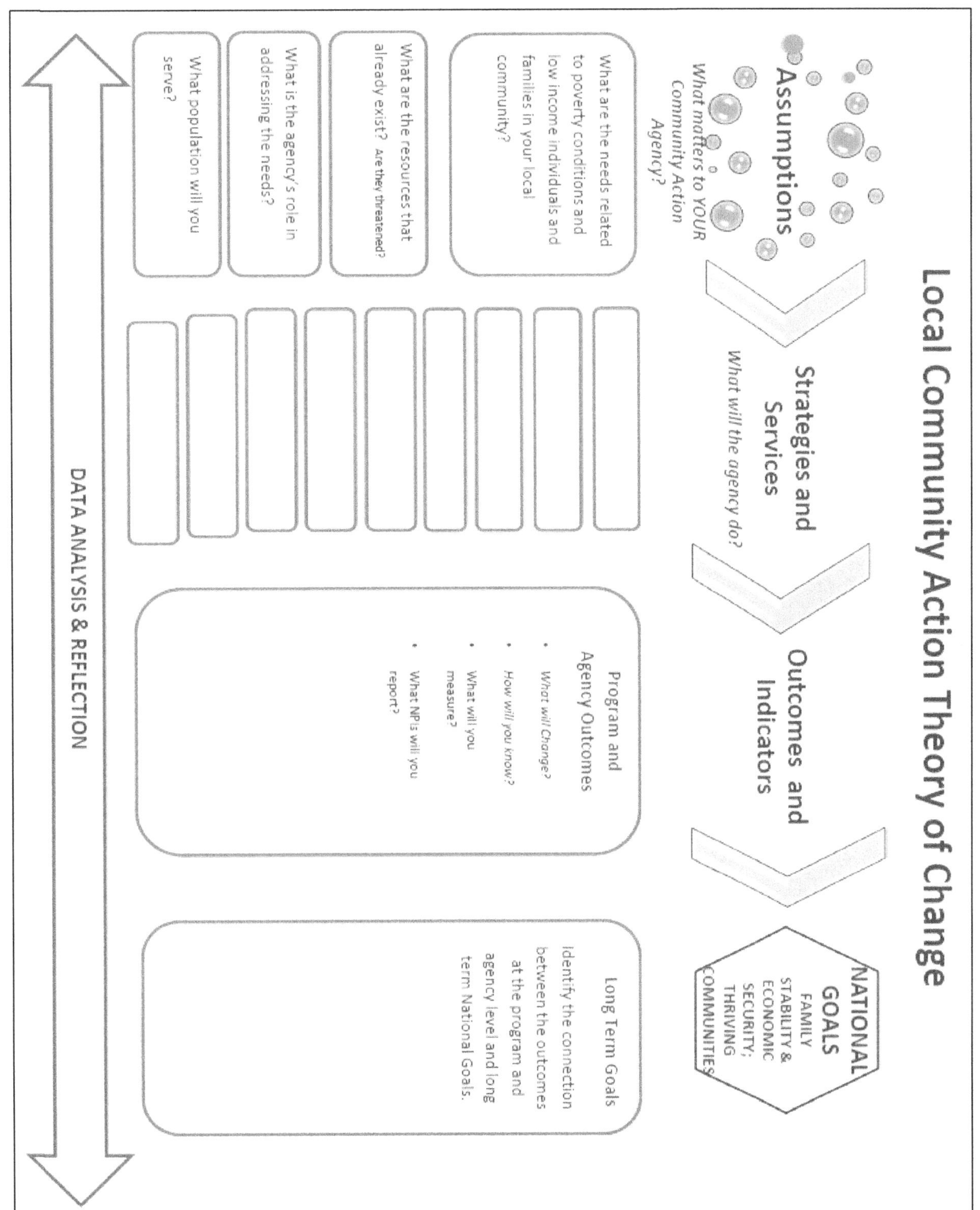

This Local TOC Template is from NASCSP publication:
Guide to Creating a Local Theory of Change, 2017, *www.nascsp.org*

Module Two – Building Blocks

Part Two

Community Assessment

Key Points -- Module Two, Part Two

- The definition of "a community to be assessed" and the target population for the community assessment are established by the agency.

- There are many kinds of data elements that produce a comprehensive community profile.
    - A comprehensive profile includes both needs and resources.
    - The assessment includes quantitative and qualitative data.
    - There is a difference between Community Engagement; Customer Input and Customer Satisfaction data.

- Analysis of data in the assessment process leads to prioritization of needs.

- It is important to distinguish between the levels of need (Family, Agency, and Community).

- Identification of the level of need sets the path for the proper level of response.

Community Assessment

The mission statement, as we have seen, defines the agency's purpose and why it is in business. By identifying a mission statement, the agency has acknowledged one or more perceived needs in the community that it wants to work to ameliorate.

We have seen broadly stated outcomes in the mission statement in the previous segment. However, these broad statements are not sufficiently detailed to help the agency develop a strategic plan of action.

Before moving to establish the activities of the agency, you must be sure to identify and understand the specific needs and resources in the community through a comprehensive assessment.

Community Assessment is a systematic process for creating a profile of the needs and resources of a given community or target population.

It is also a way to identify the assumptions and opinions about key issues held by members of the community.

What Is a Community?

Most frequently, when we think of a "community," we think of a group of individuals who are considered together because of the place in which they live or work – thus a "community of place" or a "place-based community." Such a community can be a state, a county or group of counties in a region, a neighborhood, town, or other geographically specific place. We can identify a number of other kinds of communities, including communities of action, circumstance, inquiry, interest, position, practice, and purpose.

It is up to the agency to define its community – either by the geographical location for which it receives funding to serve or by specific portions of that geography with particular needs (e.g., neighborhood with highest number of low-income residents).

Creating a Community Profile

In the assessment process, you will be creating a community profile, which includes various ways of describing the community that you have identified.

You will want to know things about the whole population that lives in the community, as a context for your work. Because you are focused on anti-poverty work, you will also need to clearly identify the "**Population in Need**."

- For instance, it is important to know both the total number of people who live in the community and, of that total, the number who are in poverty and have low-incomes.
- It is important to know the age, ethnicity, neighborhood location, and other demographics that define the population in need.

Drucker Question Two: "Who Are Our Customers?"

Drucker identifies two types of customers:

- The primary customers who are the recipients of services and whose lives will be impacted by direct participation.
- The supporting customers who may be funders, policy makers, family members, partners, and others who have input into services.

As both of these types of customers must be assessed, they must first be identified. **Identifying your customers in the initial phase** of the Community Assessment process will help you develop a plan for collecting the appropriate data.

Drucker cautions: "Customers are never static.... The organization that is devoted to results will adapt and change as they do."

You must be aware of changing demographics related to your customers. (You can get this information from Agency Reports, which we will come back to in a few pages.)

Assessment of Needs

The assessment of community needs and resources may be thought of as a way to identify the difference between "what exists" and "what should be." Agencies gather information so that decisions can be made regarding prioritization of which needs to address and identification of outcomes that can be achieved.

This comprehensive assessment forms the link between the agency's mission and the outcomes it will achieve with its services.

What Kinds of Needs Do Communities Face?

The National Theory of Change establishes a list of domains that may be addressed by the use of CSBG funding. These have been identified as important areas related to the well-being of a community and the individuals and families who live in the community.

- Employment
- Education and Cognitive Development
- Income, Infrastructure and Asset Building
- Housing
- Health/Social Behavioral Development
- Civic Engagement and Community Involvement

Additionally, a few more domains are included in the Annual Report, Module Two, where the use of CSBG funds is identified by domain.

- Linkages (e.g. partnerships that support multiple domains)
- Agency Capacity Building*

**Note that agency capacity is included in the Annual Report, and also suggested in the foundational statement of the National Theory of Change which recognizes the need for high performing Community Action Agencies that serve the community.*

Gathering Data for Assessments

The Organizational Standards identify elements of a "Community Needs Assessment." Here is information from the instructions related to Category Three in the Organizational Standards:

> "Local control of Federal CSBG resources is predicated on regular comprehensive community assessments that take into account the breadth of community needs as well as the partners and resources available in a community to meet these needs.
>
> As a part of the community assessment, the organization collects and includes current data specific to poverty and its prevalence related to gender, age, and race/ethnicity for their service area(s). The organization collects and analyzes both qualitative and quantitative data."

So how do you create a community profile?

When you are talking about the depth and breadth of a situation, you generally look to qua<u>l</u>itative data – that is data collected from discussions (using "language"). The "l" in qualitative data is the reminder that we are referencing letters and words.

To find the scope of the problem, look to qua<u>n</u>titative data – that is data comprised of "numbers." The "n" in quantitative data is the reminder that we are referencing numbers.

A community <u>must</u> also identify what resources are available. Resources can include funds, people, and programs.

Your profile will not be complete unless you include data from your own agency reports – so you can compare this data with what you find from the broader set of data elements.

Ask People What They Think

As we consider assessing community needs, emphasis should be placed on making decisions and setting priorities based on information gathered from the people likely to be affected by the needs.

This would include both the individuals you have served AND the individuals who are eligible for your services but who have not been served. The "un-served" population-in-need may be difficult to reach in this process, but consideration of how you might do so is important.

You also want to engage others in the community to provide input.

> **Community engagement** is a dynamic relational process that facilitates communication, interaction, involvement, and exchange between an organization and a community for a range of social and organizational outcomes.

Community Engagement in the assessment process will avoid the risk of the agency addressing needs that the community doesn't agree they have.

It will form the basis of future support for the activities of the agency to address commonly accepted needs.

We sometimes hear that the work of forging a consensus among stakeholders (primary and secondary customers) is too messy and time consuming and might undermine the agency's efforts. But without including the voices of the community in the assessment process, the efforts of the agency may not be supported and may even be resisted.

Customer Input and Customer Satisfaction

<u>Drucker Question Three:</u> "What Does the Customer Value?"

"The question, 'What do customers value? What satisfies their needs, wants, and aspirations?' is so complicated that it can only be answered by the customers themselves…. (p. 39)

"So begin with (your) assumptions and what you believe your customers value. Then you can compare these beliefs with what customers actually are saying, find the differences, and go on to assess your results." (p. 40)

Finding out what the customer values can **provide two kinds** of qualitative data that are important to your assessment process.

.

Customer Input

- Data that helps you identify what your customers feel they need and what they identify as needs of the community is called "**customer input.**"
  - This helps you clarify both individual/family level needs and community level needs.

Customer Satisfaction

- Data that helps you identify what is working and what needs to be improved about your agency's services is called "**customer satisfaction data**." This helps identify agency needs.
  - Customer satisfaction data can be an excellent source for identifying agency level needs as perceived by your customers. If customers are waiting a long time for service, if they can't access the services your agency has available (location or timing of offering the service), if they do not feel they are treated with respect, then all of these are things the agency will want to identify so they can dig deeper into the causes of these conditions. These questions come together to help the agency identify what it is lacking.
  - If customers are very satisfied with aspects of a service, and are reporting that they have achieved their goals, this positive feedback provides data to help the agency know what it should support, maintain or expand going forward.

*The source of the quote is, The Five Most Important Questions Self-Assessment Tool Participant Workbook, Peter F. Drucker, Third Edition, 2010.

Collecting Qualitative Data

Qualitative data is secured from asking someone what they think is important.

- Qualitative data is primarily used when you want to find the depth and breadth of an issue.
- It provides you with opinions, observations, and other rich, subtle information that you can't get any other way.
- Qualitative data can be characterized as data that uses letters.

Activity:

How would you collect qualitative data from your customers?
Customer Input?

Customer Satisfaction?

Consider the concept of "community engagement." From whom (besides your customers) would you want to get input? How would you ask them?
How would you collect qualitative data from your stakeholders?
From the general public?

Agency report data – Do your agency reports include any qualitative data?

Notes: Your customers, potential customers and the general community can be sources of both qualitative and quantitative data.

Consider the data that might be collected from surveys.
Is it qualitative or quantitative? Or both?

Collecting Quantitative Data

The other kind of data that you need to gather is <u>quantitative data.</u> This is data that will be used to add a more standardized dimension to the perceptions you have identified.

- Quantitative data provides information in specific categories, such as is often referred to as "demographic and characteristic data."
- Agency report data can also be useful to identify numbers of customers who have applied, those impacted by a particular need, and those who have achieved outcomes (and moved out of need).
- Quantitative data can be characterized as data that is presented in "numbers."

What quantitative data would you collect that might help you examine the needs of your community?

Activity:
What data would be important from state and national sources? What other sources of statistical data can you use?

What data would you collect from local sources? Identify some local sources:

Consider agency report data:
How does quantitative data from your agency reports help to create the community profile?

What specific data elements from the agency reports would be most useful?

Identifying Community Resources

When establishing a community profile, it is not sufficient to assess only needs. An important aspect of community assessment is **identifying the resources** that are **currently available** or are **being developed** to address the problems, needs, or situations in the community.

Activity: How do you gather information about these resources?

Some other things to consider:

What about resources that are threatened?

What if your customers don't identify a need because you are filling it with a specific service, but that service is threatened?

How do you identify resources that are expected to be lost to the community?

Level of Need

It is not sufficient to only identify the varying importance of the broad domain areas, as this does not provide clear identification of the perceived need facing the low-income population to be served.

(For instance, to say "Housing is the highest priority" does not help to identify the actual needs related to housing.)

Let's use the following example of different levels of need in the domain of Education. That is a broad area that would affect young children, school age children, and adults in very different ways.

The identified area of concern is high-school graduation. Consider how you can make this issue more specific by asking: "whose need it is?"

➔ You could identify this need as: "Individuals do not have high-school diplomas." The individual lacking the diploma has the need. This statement represents a family level need.

➔ You could identify the situation as it relates to the community, and articulate the need in this way: "Our community has a low high school graduation rate." This statement represents a condition that is common to the community. This is a community level need.

➔ You could think about the needs of your agency as it considers the issue of adults without high-school diploma. You might say "Our agency has a need for additional resources to establish or expand GED preparation programs for adult customers who have not graduated high school." This says the agency does not have adequate resources. This is an agency level need.

You will be able to identify other education needs in these three levels related to specific populations such as: pre-school, elementary and secondary school, adult continuing education, vocational and post-secondary education.

Activity – What Are the Needs?

Clearly identifying the needs in your community will help you understand the outcomes you want to achieve and the appropriate strategies to address the situation.

Instructions: Identify three issues, concerns, barriers, challenges, or other situations facing the individuals and families in your community, and write these below using a couple words or a sentence for each.

Be sure you identify the level of need: Is it a family, agency, or community need.

Next: Go back and number the statements (1, 2, and 3) to indicate your priority order. When you present to the group, state your #1 priority even if someone else has already stated it.

Rules:

- You cannot use one word to identify the need, as this will not help you to understand the situation because it is too broad. For instance, saying "housing" is not sufficient to identify the need.
- You cannot identify the service that you feel would address the need, but rather must consider the need that you see. For instance, saying "families need budget counseling" is focused on the service instead of the underlying need, which might be "families are unable to manage their income."
- You cannot say "It's all three levels," as this will not be helpful as you move forward. We recognize that the problems facing our communities are very complex, and probably involve multiple levels. But you are going to have to clarify the elements of the specific problem so we can all agree on the level of the need you identified.

Remember to ask yourself: Whose need is it? What is lacking?

This process, used to determine the magnitude of the needs in the community, according to "experts", is called a Key Informant Survey. The technique to identify the priorities is called a **Nominal Group Process or Consensus Method**.

Analyzing the Assessment Data

Raw data is not information.

"Raw" or "Unprocessed" data are facts, numbers or other qualitative or quantitative "elements". Raw data elements have some basic meaning but they need to be analyzed to become useful information.

Activity: How does your agency analyze the data from your assessment activities to enable you to move toward the formulation of a plan?

Here are some questions to ask to help organize the information:

- What are some of the root causes of the problem?
- Why should we be interested in the problem?
- What can be done to address the issue?
- Who should address this issue?
- Do we have control, or partial control over this issue?
- Do we have the capabilities to address the issue?
- What programs can address the issue?
- What might we change in our agency to help address the issue?
- Can we partner with someone to help address the issue?

Simple Analysis Techniques

Aggregate the Data. This means bringing the data together to organize it. There are many ways to aggregate data elements. Consider the TYPE of data to aggregate:

- Population characteristics, well-being indicators, services received

Consider HOW you will aggregate the data:

- By domain, geographic considerations, demographics

Count the number of some element that is important to you such as:

- How many live in a certain area?
- How many of a certain characteristic? (such as: age, income, etc.)
- What is the status of housing or employment opportunities? How many units or jobs are available?
- What is the scope of certain crimes in the community?
- How many responded about a specific topic?
- How many were successful (achieved an outcome)?

Compare data elements to begin to see relationships that might increase knowledge of need and changing needs such as:

- Relationship between general population and population in need.
- Changes in demographics from year to year.
- Differences between this community and state/national counts.
- Differences within groups, between two groups or among several.
- Resources available in different neighborhoods.
- Indicators of well-being in different areas of the community.

Identify possible trends. Is there a pattern in the data? For this you may also want to look at the data elements as they were presented in prior years.

- Is something improving or declining?
- Are neighborhoods changing?
- Are resources changing?

These analysis techniques may uncover unexpected relationships that might help you to better understand the issues and improve your results.

Identify Agency Priorities

There are numerous methods to identify which issues in your community have risen to the top of the list and ways to decide which issues the agency could address.

In a previous activity, (What are the Community Needs?) we did a quick prioritization activity by counting the number of people who agreed that a stated need was the top priority for the agency to address using the **"nominal group process"** or "**consensus method**" of identifying a priority.

But this isn't the only way to identify the priority needs that your agency will address.

<u>Consider Mission:</u> What if all of the data points to a situation that is not a part of your agency mission?

<u>Consider Resources:</u> What if you have no resources to address the situation?

A few other techniques available:

- ➔ Identify Root Causes/The Five Whys
- ➔ Force Field Analysis
- ➔ Comparison techniques
- ➔ Cause and effect
- ➔ Trend Analysis

Assess What Must Be Strengthened or Abandoned

When you attempt to prioritize the needs that will be addressed in the *next planning cycle*, it is important to identify what has been accomplished related to the needs assessed by the agency *in the prior period*. Use your agency report data to consider what needs were addressed by your services and strategies, and what outcomes were achieved.

If we discover that we have not produced the intended results, we must consider if the need is still present and if it is still a priority. Consider the following:

- Is there something in the current assessment process that might shed additional light on the need situation?
- Is there something else happening that was not previously identified?

Then decide if the service you were providing should be abandoned or strengthened. The primary questions are: Did we make headway on the identified need? Can we justify putting our resources in this area going forward?

The agency must be careful to distinguish between programs and services that are not achieving outcomes to meet a need (i.e., those that should no longer be a part of the agency's range of services), and those services that are essential to your mission but are currently not producing outstanding results.

Some things must be abandoned:

"Need alone does not justify continuing. Nor does tradition… People in any organization are attached to the obsolete, things that should have worked but did not, things that once were productive and no longer are."

(p. 43) Drucker Self Assessment Workbook, 1999

Some things must be strengthened:

"If essential performance areas are weak, they must be strengthened..." by committing more resources to address the need.

(p. 44) Drucker Self Assessment Workbook, 1999

Activity – What Is Our Family Level Need?

During this Introduction to ROMA we are considering the fundamental principles related to the performance management of a local agency – including needs at all three levels.

However, for the purposes of this basic curriculum, we are building a **family level** logic model.

Work at community and agency levels will require a bit of a twist on the family level logic model, and information about these can be found in supplemental materials.

Activity: Select the top priority family level need from the activity done earlier in this module. Be sure to correctly identify the need (not a need for a service)

Note: In the Intro to ROMA Training, we are building a family level logic model.

Family Level Logic Model

1	2	3	4	5	6	7	8
N							
Mission:							

Module Two Review

1. The key elements of a good mission statement are:

2. Why is understanding the assumptions behind mission statements important?

3. Two times when a mission should be changed are:

4. What is the value of a Local Theory of Change?

5. Who defines the community that your agency will assess?

6. What kinds of data are included in the Community Needs Assessment (CNA) document?

7. Describe how a survey can produce both qualitative and quantitative data.

8. What is the value of including agency report data in the CNA?

9. Please identify the level of need represented by the statements below:
   - Individuals lack skills to secure living wage jobs (   )
   - There are no living wage jobs available (   )
   - We do not provide job training programs (   )

10. What do you want to consider to help you know if your efforts in a particular area should be abandoned or strengthened?

Module Three

Developing Results-Oriented Plans

Part One
Introduction to Planning

Part Two
Identifying Outcomes

Part Three
Identifying Outputs

Module Three

Developing Results-Oriented Plans

Part One - Introduction to Planning

Key Points – Module Three, Part One

- A clear process is important to manage an agency through the implementation, evaluation, reassessment and revision of a plan.
- Planning is one of the activities identified in the Community Action Organizational Standards.
- The agency Board of Directors has an important role in the planning process and is responsible for approval of the final product that guides the policies of the agency going forward.
- There is a difference between an Agency-Wide Strategic Plan, the Community Action Plan and other department plans.
- The use of its mission statement and local Theory of Change can help identify what the agency wants to accomplish at family, agency and community levels.
- Agency plans must connect to the needs identified and prioritized in the assessment process.

Activity – Why Plan?

Instructions: **Think about why planning is part of the ROMA Cycle. Write your ideas below.**

What Comes First?

We propose that this is NOT the way to seek funding or to allocate resources in your agency.

Rather, you should decide how each funding source and other resources can <u>support your mission to meet an identified need.</u>

You also need to consider how *all the agency resources* taken together will <u>produce the outcome(s) you wish to achieve.</u>

What Is Our Plan?

<u>Drucker Question Five:</u> "What Is Our Plan?"

Drucker tells us that the written plan will help us "get the right things done." He also reminds us of the importance of **involving the agency Board of Directors.** *The following quotes are from the Drucker Self Assessment Workbook, 1999*

"The self-assessment process leads to a plan that is a concise summation of the organization's purpose and future direction….The development and formal adoption of mission and goals are fundamental to effective governance of a nonprofit organization and are primary responsibilities of the board. Therefore these strategic elements of the plan must be **approved by the Board**." (p. 65)

"The most difficult challenge is to agree on the institution's goals – the fundamental long-range direction. Goals flow from the mission, aim the organization where it must go, build on strength, address opportunity, and take together, outline your desired future." (p.66)

"True self-assessment is never finished. Leadership requires that constant resharpening, refocusing, never really being satisfied." (p. 56*)

The written plan isn't about having strategies and outcomes fixed for all time in a document, but about proving the ability for the Board to continuously refer back to the plan as the agency moves forward with implementation. Plan documents must be reviewed, and can be revised if changes are needed to achieve the agency goals.

Note: Referring back to the plan throughout the ROMA Cycle allows the agency to:

- review and appraise the value of each element,
- identify elements needed for implementation of services and strategies,
- update the elements as new data is collected and analyzed,
- reflect community changes around you.

Different Types of Plans

The **Agency-Wide Strategic Plan** includes the vision and direction set by the board for the entire agency.

The **Community Action Plan** is a work plan which identifies how CSBG funds are used – both to fund activities provided directly by the agency and as leverage for additional support for the anti-poverty work the agency is doing.

Proposals or other formal requests to funding sources that have specific population and outcome focus, also become agency plans when they are successful. These provide other resources to supplement the work that cannot be done with the CSBG funding alone.

This book shelf is like the CAA's Agency-Wide Strategic Plan.

Think of the Community Action Plan as one of the books on the shelf, and other funding proposals as other books.

Community Action Plan

To comply with the Community Services Block Grant (CSBG) Act, Public Law 105-285, Section 678B (11) eligible entities must complete a Community Action Plan (CAP), as a condition to receive funding through a Community Services Block Grant.

- The CAP must reflect how CSBG funds are to be utilized to support activities that remove obstacles and solve problems that block the achievement of self-sufficiency.
- The CAP is part of the contract process for the State in determining how CSBG funds are used by local eligible entities.
- While it is a road map for the use of CSBG funds, the CAP also is to include the other activities the agency plans to offer in a comprehensive and effective continuum of programs and services for individuals, families and communities with low income that may be supported by various funding for each program or service.

PUBLIC LAW 105–285—OCT. 27, 1998

This builds on earlier guidance:

OEO Instructions (1970):
"CAAs must develop both a long-range strategy and specific, short-range plans for using potential resources… In developing its strategy and plans, the CAA shall take into account the areas of greatest community need, the availability of resources, and its own strengths and limitations."

CSBG Policy Issuance #98-9.13 (3/30/98)
"Beginning in FY 1999, the CAP Plan has been revised...divided into three sections: (A) Community Needs Assessment, (B) Service Delivery System, and (C) Addressing Community Needs. *Section C includes information on Annual Performance Measures, Self Sufficiency Case Management and Community Revitalization."*

Agency-Wide Strategic Plan

- Agencies may have a mission that is broader than a focus on anti-poverty strategies, and they use funding sources that allow for the agency to have a broader customer base.
- While the CAP may identify multiple funding sources that are being leveraged to provide services to individuals, families, and communities with low income, the agency's Strategic Plan will also include resources for the broader customer base.

Strategic Thinking is:

Thinking big: Do we understand how we connect and intersect with other organizations and the external environment? Think about the larger systems of which we are a part.

Thinking deeply: How deeply are we questioning the way we do things today? Do we operate from our interpretation of the past, or our anticipation of the future? Will our assumptions today be valid into the future?

Think of the future: How far into the future are we looking? Do we understand the shape of alternative futures for our organizations? Or, do we expect tomorrow will be more of today?

Strategic Thinking: what it is and how to do it. Available from: https://www.researchgate.net/publication/253238955_Strategic_Thinking_what_it_is and_how_to_do_it [accessed Sep 21, 2017].

Guidance from Organizational Standards

The Organizational Standards related to local CAA Planning activities, echo the understanding that the Community Action Agency is more than just CSBG funded activities.

From the introduction to the Planning Standards:

"Establishing the vision for a Community Action Agency is a big task and setting the course to reach it through strategic planning is serious business. CSBG eligible entities take on this task by looking both at internal functioning and at the community's needs. An efficient organization knows where it is headed, how the board and staff fit into that future, and how it will measure its success in achieving what it has set out to do. This agency-wide process is board-led and ongoing. A "living, breathing" strategic plan with measurable outcomes is the goal, rather than a plan that gets written but sits on a shelf and stagnates. Often set with an ambitious vision, strategic plans set the tone for the staff and board and are a key leadership and management tool for the organization."

The first three Standards in the section identify some characteristics of the Strategic Plan:

- **Standard 6.1** The organization has an agency-wide strategic plan in place that has been approved by the governing board within the past 5 years.

- **Standard 6.2** The approved strategic plan addresses reduction of poverty, revitalization of low-income communities, and/or empowerment of people with low incomes to become more self-sufficient.

- **Standard 6.3** The approved strategic plan contains family, agency, and/or community goals.

Module Three

Developing Results-Oriented Plans

Part Two - Identifying Outcomes

Key Points – Module Three, Part Two

- Community Action Agencies plan for outcomes.

- There are different kinds of outcomes:
  - Those that recognize time, direction, and status;
  - Those that identify short, intermediate and long term outcomes.

- Outcomes are identified on Family, Agency and Community levels and must match the level of need.

- Outcomes must be appropriately matched to stated needs.

What Are Our Results?

Drucker Question Four: "What Are Our Results?"

Drucker advises us that the results of social sector organizations are measured outside the organization in changed lives and changed conditions. He says that we should look at both "short term accomplishments and long term change." *(p. 40*)*

According to Drucker, "in business you can debate whether profit is really an adequate measuring stick, but without it there is no business in the long term. In the social sector, no such universal standard for success exists. Each organization must identify its customers ...and honestly judge whether lives are being changed." *(p. 41*)*

** Page numbers refer to the Drucker Self-Assessment Workbook, 1999*

It is up to each agency to identify their successes and assure that they have clear documentation ("evidence") of the success. When these successes are reported to the state and federal CSBG offices using a common set of National Performance Indicators, we can begin to understand the common results being achieved across the country.

Results or Outcomes? Changes!

We use the word "results" and the word "outcomes" interchangeably as we move through the various principles in this manual. Simply put, outcomes or results are changes observed or reported after participation in a service or activity. CAAs and CSBG Eligible Entities, whether private nonprofit community-based organizations or agencies of local government (that provide direct services and/or use subcontractors), produce outcomes for individuals, families, their community, and the agency itself.

- **For the family,** outcomes are changes in knowledge, attitudes, skill or ability, or behavior.
- **For the agency and community,** outcomes may be such things as changes in agency or public policy, organizational effectiveness, or social and health conditions.

Types of Outcomes

Outcomes may happen over time, may represent a change in the situation or status, or may be a change in direction for the family, agency, or community.

Change Over Time:

You will identify the change you plan to observe, in a time frame that matches the situation. This may be characterized as Short-term, Intermediate, or Long-term. Time frames differ with different situations.

Example: Short-term for a family in need of shelter may be "this afternoon," while short-term for someone obtaining basic job skills training may be six months.

Change in Status:

A change in status (or condition) is a change in one of many variables that we use to determine if a situation is getting better or worse. Situations may be identified at different levels of status that are related to the perceptions of those in the situation regarding need for action/intervention. Thriving is a status that is generally accepted as "well-being" while being a state of "in-crisis" indicates urgency for action.

Example: Residents of one public housing project may feel they are safe, while those in another project might feel they are in-crisis, depending on the location, neighbors, and other environmental factors. Other housing situations can be considered thriving.

Change in Direction:

A positive outcome indicates progress toward a goal.

A negative outcome may indicate that the situation has changed for the worse.

Positive and negative are not the same as "increase" and "decrease" which are terms often used in outcome language. Some outcomes are those that you want to decrease (such as the rate of teen pregnancy) and that decrease would be a positive outcome.

A neutral outcome may indicate stability or no change in status.

This kind of outcome can be expected when we are assisting a family to maintain a stable situation. It can also mean that the family is not making progress or movement toward a goal. These are different kinds of neutral outcomes.

Examples of Family Outcomes

A primary goal of Community Action Agencies is to help families become self-sufficient, stable or economically secure – i.e. to be able to care for all of their family needs without assistance.

Many times, the family must first become stable before they can move on to achieve this goal.

These examples are family level outcomes; some are about individuals and others are about the entire family.

- Individuals increased knowledge, improved education level or skills.
- Individuals gained a diploma or certificate.
- Parents increased family functioning skills.
- Individuals increased ability to manage income.
- Individuals increased ability to accumulate and use assets.
- Families obtained, maintained, or improved housing arrangements.
- Families obtained adequate, safe, affordable, unsubsidized, permanent housing.
- Families avoided utility shut off or had utilities reconnected.
- Individuals improved or maintained nutrition.
- Individuals improved or maintained physical or behavioral health.
- Children and youth achieved expected growth and development.
- Senior citizens and individuals with disabilities maintained independent living.
- Households increased income:
    - From employment:
        - Unemployed persons obtained employment or self-employment.
        - Employed persons obtained better employment or self-employment.
        - Employed persons maintained employment for at least 90 days.
    - From non-employment sources:
        - Custodial parent secured support from non-custodial parent,
        - Family secured tax credit refund.

This is a list of possible outcomes at the Family level.
It is not meant to be all inclusive.

Examples of Community Outcomes

Community outcomes are an integral part of Community Action and describe the allocation and focusing of public and private resources for antipoverty purposes, improvement in the community infrastructure, and creation of opportunities and resources to support low-income people in their transition towards self-sufficiency.

Community outcomes may include increased quality of life, policy changes to support movement out of poverty, or other changes that impact the profile of the community.

- Communities, in which people with low-income live, improved access to essential services.
- The supply of affordable housing is increased.
- The number of job opportunities, particularly living wage jobs, is increased.
- Community facilities are established, renovated, or otherwise maintained.
- Financial services, access to capital and available lending programs were increased.
- Transportation resources are increased.
- Education resources are increased.
- Municipal infrastructure was maintained or improved.

This is a list of possible outcomes at the Community level.
It is not meant to be all inclusive.

Examples of Agency Outcomes

Agencies that are well run and meet accepted standards of excellence demonstrate continuous improvement and capacity to meet the needs of low-income individuals/families and communities.

It is important to identify agency goals to assure the agency capacity to achieve results is maintained.

- Increased resources (including in-kind and donated resources).
- Increased/maintained sufficient discretionary funding to support unexpected negative cash flow.
- Acquired or maintained a common intake system that tracks customers across all agency programs.
- Increased ability to document customer achievement of outcomes.
- Improved implementation of the full range of ROMA activities.
- Board monitored and improved functioning to support an active tripartite Board as described in IM 82.
- Increased or maintained fiscal management that includes adherence to generally accepted accounting practices.
- Programs achieved accreditation demonstrating that programs obtained a level of excellence or met or exceeded nationally recognized standards.
- Staff has appropriate credentials for their job functions.
- Staff has qualifications needed for specific activities.
- Agency's strategic planning efforts include both staff and Board.
- The agency has documentation of increased use of data in planning and decision making.
- Met 90% of the Organizational Standards.

This is a list of possible outcomes at the Agency level.
It is not meant to be all inclusive.

Comparison of Outcomes for Employment

Previously we identified needs to be assessed in three levels: Family, Agency, and Community.

Consider the outcomes that are achieved in those same three levels in the Employment domain example below:

Family *employment* outcomes can address an individual's employment status such as:

- Secured employment (full-time, part-time, self-employment).
- Improved earnings from income (or received additional benefits).
- Retained employment.

Agency *employment* outcomes can address the capacity of the CAA to achieve results for its customers.

- Improved resources to provide job training and employment placement for people with low-incomes.
- Agency staff has adequate job coaching skills.

Community *employment* outcomes can address factors that affect the ability to secure/maintain employment, as well as employment conditions:

- Additional public transportation routes were created or timing of the routes was adapted (increasing access to jobs for people with low-incomes).
- Second-shift childcare opportunities for people with low-incomes were created or expanded.
- Increase in job opportunities.
- Unemployment rate decreased.

While many social sector organizations help people find employment, CAAs also create jobs, reduce barriers, leverage funds for training, and contribute to the overall economy and economic development of the community.

Examples of Community Engagement Outcomes

Some outcomes are specifically focused on improving the participation of people with low-incomes in community organizations and community activities.

They include different levels of outcomes – some at the community level (indicators of positive community change and stability), some at the family level (as they are about the person with low income achieving something), and some at the agency level (when the activities of persons with low income assist to expand the capacity of the agency to provide services and engage in strategies).

- People with low-incomes opened or maintained a business.
- People with low-incomes purchased a home.
- People with low-incomes secured a role in formal community organizations, government offices, community boards or councils that provide input for decision-making and reflect the needs of the low-income community.
- Community Action program participants increased skills, knowledge, and abilities to enable them to work with Community Action to improve conditions in the community.
- Community Action program participants improved their leadership skills and assumed leadership positions in the community.
- Community Action program participants improved their social networks.
- Volunteer participation of people with low-incomes increased the capacity of the community (or the agency) to meet needs:
    - Increased numbers of participants who could be served
    - Extended hours or added locations of service
- The number and scope of opportunities for people with low-incomes to participate in advocacy activities resulting in policy and program change increased.
- Leadership opportunities available in the community for people with low-incomes increased.

This is a list of possible Community Engagement outcomes.
It is not meant to be all inclusive.

Activity – What Is the Outcome?

The outcome you want to achieve must be directly related to the identified need. Correctly matching the outcome to the need also includes being sure the level of the outcome (family, agency, community) is the same as the level of the need.

Instructions: Identify the outcome that could be achieved that matches the stated need.

NEED	OUTCOME
1. Individuals need transportation to get to work.	
2. Staff lacks skills to work with families in trauma.	
3. There is not cnough affordable housing in our community.	
4. Families need housing they can afford.	
5. We do not have a housing program at our agency.	
6. Individuals need skills to prepare them for living wage jobs.	
7. Children are not ready for school.	
8. Senior citizens have homes that are in disrepair, which threatens independence.	
9. Families report food scarcity at least once a month.	
10. There are no summer feeding programs in this community.	

Activity – Family Level Outcomes

<u>Instructions:</u> Identify outcomes your agency can work to achieve at the family level.

Consider the needs identified in Module 2. The needs and outcomes must match.

Note: In the Intro to ROMA Training, we are building a family level logic model.

Family Level Logic Model

1	2	3	4	5	6	7	8
N		O					
Mission:							

Module Three

Developing Results-Oriented Plans

Part Three - Identifying Outputs

Key Points – Module Three, Part Three

- There is an important difference between outcomes and outputs.
- "Provision of Services" and "Strategic Thinking" models each contain unique assumptions that could be reflected in the agency's Local Theory of Change (LTOC).
- The Mission/Local TOC, Assessment of Needs and Resources, and Identification of Outcomes are driving forces in the selection of strategies and services.
- Proxy Outcomes can be used in appropriate situations to stand in for actual outcomes.

Connecting Need, Outcomes, and Services/Strategies

We have seen how the agency's mission statement is the foundation upon which all plans for services must be built. Actions must also be designed to meet specific needs – identified on the family, agency, or community level. These actions must be designed to achieve the specific outcomes you/the agency plan to achieve by matching the appropriate family, agency, or community need.

But what are the next actions to be undertaken by the agency?

The agency must select services and strategies to achieve the desired outcomes. **Services** are what are directly provided to an individual or family. Agency and community **strategies** can include resource development, capacity building, advocacy activities, and other actions.

Consider the "plan" developed by this group:

Don't rely on "magic" as a strategy when you make your plan!

You must start with the knowledge of what you want to achieve, identify the resources you have or can bring to the project, and then clearly lay out the services, strategies, advocacy efforts, and other interventions you will implement.

Provision of Services and Strategic Thinking

Community Action Agencies are more than service providers. As the agency considers what it will do with available resources targeted to achieving the identified outcomes for families, communities, or the agency, will it be a "service provider," "self-sufficiency/anti-poverty agent," or both? The agency's service delivery practices are reflected in the agency core assumptions about their purpose in anti-poverty work.

PROVISION OF SERVICES MODEL	STRATEGIC THINKING MODEL
Agencies that are organized to meet specific single or short-term services (such as emergency services, transportation, and weatherization) are able to serve <u>many customers</u> and meet an immediate need. **The <u>challenge</u> is being able to identify <u>long-term change</u> the service produced has in the customers' lives.** A single service will have <u>limited impact</u> in addressing the complex situation facing most families with low-income. **Providing services because funding is available can distract you from a <u>more effective selection</u> of services and strategies.** Sometimes there are <u>unintended consequences</u> of doing the same services you always have done: *enabling the continuation of poverty.*	**The development of comprehensive strategies reflects understanding of the power of "bundling services."** Agencies can <u>identify the combination of services</u> that are most effective for helping to change lives and support movement out of poverty. **Receipt of several services together is more likely to move someone to improved status than a service that meets an isolated need.** This increased intensity means that <u>fewer customers</u> are served. **Strategic thinking requires agencies to look beyond provision of direct services to individuals and families.** They must explore the impact of creating <u>community engagement</u> strategies, <u>advocacy</u> and <u>policy change</u> strategies, and other activities that are focused on reduction of poverty. And they must strengthen <u>partnerships</u> to meet the needs that the agency cannot address alone.

Activity – Pros and Cons of Both Models

Identify the strengths and the challenges of the "Provision of Services" and "Strategic Thinking" models in the chart below.

Model:	Pros	Cons
Provision of Services		
Strategic Thinking		

The agency's service delivery practices are reflected in the agency's Local Theory of Change. At the local level your agency will want to demonstrate:

- How well it operates
- What difference it makes

Consider the "Strategic Thinking" approach in conjunction with the concepts raised in Module Two when we introduced Local Theories of Change. Using the Strategic Thinking model will help you build a Local Theory of Change by considering the whole agency and not just the activities that are funded through CSBG, and also considering the engagement of your low-income customers and the community at large.

The Local TOC, along with the agency mission statement, are driving forces in the selection of services and strategies that will be implemented with agency resources in the coming year.

Services and Strategies

The core activities for Eligible Entities, identified in Information Memorandum 49, includes:

- Strategies that use existing resources and develop new ones to address needs.
- The relationship of activities supported by the Agency to other anti-poverty, community development services in community.
- The extent Agency activities contribute to the accomplishment of one or more of the national ROMA goals.

This means that Community Action Agencies should be considering activities that will produce **family and community level** outcomes.

In the CSBG Annual Report, agencies have the opportunity to report on these activities as separate from the outcomes related to the National Performance Indicators.

The report's **community level strategies** and **family level services** establish a menu of activities that are indicative of the various approaches different CAAs use to ameliorate the anti-poverty mission.

In this Introduction to ROMA session, we focus on family level services as we discuss outputs. Community level (and agency level) strategies will be a part of future training. However, the distinction between outputs and outcomes found on the following pages are also applied to community and agency level work.

The outcomes are the changes and the outputs are the activities.

Outputs – What We Do!

When we talk about the process of the service, the quantity of the work produced by the service or other qualifiers regarding the service, we are talking about "outputs."

Think of other places where the term "output" is used. You hear about the audio or video output of your computer, the artistic output of a painter, or the output of a factory. In these cases, the term can be thought of as the quantity of what is being produced. It can also refer to the production process itself.

Outputs are the activities of the program – both the activities of the provider (the CAA or partners) and the activities of the customers.

Family level outputs are measured by such things as units of service, number of people served, number of households or families served, amount of service received (hours, dollars, or other measure), hours of participation, or number of times in attendance at a program or activity.

Measuring outputs will provide data regarding the scope of the program, but it will not tell you what changes happened to the customers.

Outcomes and Outputs

CAAs are held accountable for producing outcomes, AND they also must demonstrate they have the capacity to achieve their results through effective and efficient management and delivery of services and strategies.

It is important that we acknowledge that when we provide a service, this service is not the same as a change that happens to the customer as a result of the service. The service is what we call the output. Deciding which elements of the program are outputs and which are outcomes is important for both management and accountability. We must be clear about the difference.

Output	Outcome
The adult customer participates in a training program.	The adult will increase skills.
The family receives utility assistance.	The family will avoid a utility shut off.
The child attends Head Start.	The child will be ready for school.

Sometimes there is a question – such as when customers are participating in a service but there is no documented measurable *change in knowledge or skills*. Some want to count participation (attendance) as an outcome. However, to be truly "results oriented," you must actually identify a *change in behavior*, e.g., improved hygiene, use of appropriate dress, being able to keep to a schedule.

Output	Outcome
Customer participation/attendance	Change in behavior

On the following page, you will find examples of various elements of programs typically offered by Community Action Agencies. Please consider if these elements are outcomes or outputs. If you cannot identify what has changed, then the item is probably an output, not an outcome.

Activity – Outcomes and Outputs

Instructions: The statements below contain both outcomes and outputs for each of the programs. In the space provided, please write the letters "OC" for outcome and the letters "OP" for output.

Adult Basic Education (A.B. E.)

OP Outreach and recruitment
OP Enrolls in A.B.E. class
OP Attends A.B.E. classes
OP Completes A.B.E. classes (meets attendance requirements) – A change is not noted
OC Achieves competency in basic math, reading, and writing skills
OC Receives certificate or diploma

Employment

OP Outreach and recruitment
OP Enrolls in employability counseling
OC Completes apprenticeship and masters a skill
OC Offered employment after successful interview
OC Obtained part-time employment
OC Obtained full-time employment
OC Maintains employment for 90 days

Emergency Assistance

___ Obtained bag of food
___ Alleviated hunger
___ Obtained one month emergency rent payment
___ Able to stay in apartment
___ Prevented homelessness
___ Received check for utility bill
___ Electric service not shut off
___ Received a referral to childcare

Weatherization

___ New furnace installed in home
___ Homes insulated to R-18
___ Kitchen appliances repaired or replaced
___ New thermostat installed
___ Electric utilization, kkw decreased by 10%
___ Gas consumption ccf, decreased by 10%
___ Arrearages eliminated
___ Energy expenditures reduced
___ Value of house rises

Conflict Management

___ Youths are involved in fewer conflicts
___ Discussion sessions explore experiences with stereotyping, cultural differences
___ Youth display greater tolerance of differing points of view
___ Youth practice communication and negotiation skills
___ Youth report more willingness to have friends with backgrounds different from theirs

After School

___ Children master new activities
___ Fifteen (15) at-risk children attend after school sessions
___ Activities are designed to encourage cooperative play
___ Children's social skills improve
___ Children make more positive use of free time outside the program

Parent Education

___ Parents from 10 families attend workshops
___ Six group workshops are conducted
___ Parents' understanding of children's developmental issues increases
___ Parents provide more age-appropriate guidance to children
___ Parents participate in role plays and group discussion

Tutoring

___ Twenty (20) children in grades 4 to 8 are matched with high school tutors
___ Children's academic performance increases
___ Children indicate increased belief in their abilities to learn new subjects
___ Children receive one-to-one help in reading and math
___ Tutors emphasize the importance of Education

The Exception to the Rule: Proxy Outcomes

In some special situations, the receipt of a service may be assumed to be the achievement of an outcome. It may not be practical for your agency to measure or collect outcome data, but others have collected data and validated the connection between the service and the outcome. **In this situation the output can "stand in" for an outcome and is called a "proxy" for an actual outcome.**

A proxy outcome may be used when these conditions are present:

- An identified actual outcome is supported by previous research and, because of the established research, the outcome is recognized and accepted to be related to the service.
- The individual is eligible for the intervention, activity, or service because of an identified risk factor and the research shows that those with the eligibility requirements who participate will yield the expected outcome(s).

Example: If a senior citizen receives a home-delivered or congregate meal (output), you assume that the person has reduced hunger (outcome) or increased nutrition (outcome).

It would be impractical for you to actually test to assure "reduced hunger" or "increased nutrition" has occurred. Fortunately, there is sufficient research data to support these outcomes for those individuals who are eligible to participate in congregate or home delivered meal programs. This research determines that a specific group of individuals who are at risk of negative behaviors would benefit from the program and achieve some, if not all, of the expected outcomes as described in the supporting research.

The count of the number of people who received meals is the proxy for outcomes that cannot be realistically measured (such as "reduced hunger") NOT the number of meals provided.

Use of Proxy Outcomes

Another Example: After-School Programs

- If you provide an after school program that includes a homework helper component, you should be able to identify an improvement in grades for students who attend; or an improvement in school behavior. These would be the measurable outcomes for the program.

- Research shows that after school programs also impact on the reduction of juvenile crime and the reduction of teen pregnancies (considered to be negative behaviors). These are real outcomes, but local programs cannot document that they prevented something from happening. The research provides the documentation that shows the connection and can prove prevention of negative behaviors. Therefore, measuring attendance/participation in these situations is considered an acceptable proxy for the other outcomes.

- The count of the number of students who are part of the targeted at-risk population who attended the program could be a proxy for the number of students who reduced negative behavior.

When research supports the causative relationship between the service provided to a specific population that has been identified as being at-risk, and an identified outcome, then the number of individuals receiving the service becomes a proxy outcome, counted "in place of" the actual outcome.

Remember:

- Identification of attendance or receipt of a service as a proxy outcome is not to be accepted or used without proper supporting research and can only be applied to the targeted at-risk population.
- If you can measure the outcome easily, a proxy outcome is not appropriate, because you have an actual outcome. In the after-school program example, if you are able to track improved grades or behavior, these would be actual outcomes of the program.

Activity – Assumptions Behind Services

We've already looked at the assumptions found in mission statements. Similarly, there are assumptions behind the selection of services and strategies in which the agency engages.

These are activities that have been reported from the Community Action Network. Consider each of these and what the agency might believe that would suggest that these activities would produce results.

This is what the agency did:	What assumptions do you see?
Provide budget counseling to people who are deeply in debt	
Distribute monthly food boxes	
Create a community coalition to work with employers who do not give jobs to local residents	

Every time the agency selects a service or strategy that will take planning, identification of resources and staff involvement, they are bringing their assumptions into play – even if they do not acknowledge the assumptions.

Activity – Family Level Services

Instructions: Consider the needs identified in Module 2 and the outcomes you identified earlier in this module.

What direct services for individuals and families can your agency implement to achieve the outcomes and meet the needs?

Note: In the Intro to ROMA Training, we are building a family level logic model.

Family Level Logic Model

1	2	3	4	5	6	7	8
N	S	O					
Mission:							

Module Three Review

Please circle True or False, or fill in the blank.

1. An agency-wide strategic plan is required in the Organizational Standards. True or False

2. Once the agency's Strategic Plan is approved by the Board, it cannot be changed for 3 years. True or False

3. A community action plan is required as a means to secure CSBG funding. True or False

4. The term "Outputs" is the same as the term "Results." True or False

5. An outcome may be short, ________________, or ______________ term.

6. Which of the following can be dimensions of an outcome (circle all that apply):
   a. Time
   b. Direction
   c. Status
   d. Services

7. It is important to match the level of need and the level of outcome because:____

8. The Provision of Services model has too many challenges to allow it to be a viable operating principle in a local CAA. True or False

9. A Proxy Outcome is acceptable when: (circle all that apply)
   a. Research has been done with a specific target at-risk population to verify the relationship between a service and an outcome.
   b. The agency does not have time to do follow up.
   c. It is obvious that the service helps the recipient.

10. Attendance at a program for adults seeking a high school diploma is an example of a Proxy Outcome. True or False

Module Four

Implementing the Plan

Key Points – Module Four:

- It is important to appraise the plan prior to implementation.
- Reginald Carter's Seven Key Questions can be used to support management of services.
- Outcome Indicators add specificity to the general Outcome statements.
- Outcome indicators compare the service provided to customers with the success of the customer in achieving outcomes.
- The National Performance Indicators are a standard set of indicators found in the CSBG Annual Report that are most commonly achieved by Community Action Agencies across the country.

Implementing the Plan

A well written plan leads to sound agency management and accountability… provided the plan is well implemented.

Drucker cautions us:

"Work doesn't get done by a magnificent statement of policy. Work is only done when it is done. Done by people. By people who are properly informed, assigned and equipped."

"The nonprofit organization must be information-based. Information must flow from the individuals doing the work to the board management, and it must flow back as well."

"What we measure and how we measure it determines what will be considered relevant and thereby determines not just what we see but what we and others do."

Drucker Self Assessment Workbook, 1999, p 59 and 60

We have help from Reginald Carter with some questions to guide us as we consider how we will implement our plan.

As we move forward to implementation of our services and strategies, we must understand what gets put into operation to achieve and document results. These include:

- Identifying the fundamental elements necessary for implementation.
- Identifying procedures (including measurement and storage tools) and personnel for observation and reporting of results.

Reginald Carter's Seven Key Questions

Dr. Reginald Carter used his experiences as the Director of Planning and Evaluation for the Michigan Department of Social Services as the basis for writing ***The Accountable Agency (1983).*** [1]

Carter states that each year when a program manager presents a budget for services to be implemented, there are seven questions that should be asked. He proposed that all agencies should be able to answer these seven questions in order to justify the budget amounts that will support the activities of the agency.

You should be able to answer these questions as you begin to implement your plan.

1. **How many clients are you serving?**
2. **Who are they?**
3. **What services do you give them?**
4. What does it cost?
5. What does it cost per service delivered?
6. **What happens to the clients as a result of the service?**
7. What does it cost per outcome?

We will focus on questions 1, 2, 3, and 6 that identify the clients/customers, the services which are provided and the expected outcomes. These are essential elements to implementing any plan.

These questions also frame criteria for accountability that include both efficiency and effectiveness measures.

---

[1] © The Accountable Agency, Reginald Carter, Sage Human Services Guide 34, 1983. **This book is available free, downloaded at: www.appliedmgt.com.**

Carter's Key Questions

1. How many clients are you serving?

- **The number of individuals projected to be served is often based on budget and other resource data.** This projected number is important as you implement your plan.

- **Agencies must be able to provide unduplicated counts of their customers being served.** Without this ability, your customers may be counted multiple times.

If the agency does not have a common intake or common identification number, and each program or service assigns their own identification number, the agency will in all likelihood have a duplicated customer count. This is also known as a silo approach to counting customers.

To assure an unduplicated count, each person/family is considered to be a customer of the agency and not an individual program. In this method, they are assigned a single identification number, which would go along with the customer to any program or service received.

A factor that will affect how the agency counts customers:

The agency must determine **when a person/family becomes a customer**, which may vary by program. Lack of standardization about when the customer is entered into the agency system may result in duplicated counts (as identified above) but also may result in an undercount, with some programs counting every customer who filed an application and others not counting until the customer has received a minimum amount of service.

Does receipt of *any* type of service, qualify an individual as a customer in your agency? For example, if the service is "information only" or a referral, is the person a customer of the Information and Referral service of the agency? How is this individual counted, if at all?

Carter's Key Questions – Continued

2. Who are they?

- **In the plan, the agency may have identified a specific target population, based on the community assessment.**
- **Upon intake and assessment, the agency must collect basic demographic and characteristic data such as age, gender, income, employment, education, disability status, race, and ethnicity.**

This data can clarify and enrich the outcome information.

For example, information about customers could help you understand the elements that make a difference in one's ability to find and maintain a job. Is it a prior work history? Do factors of race, age, gender, neighborhood, or other factor/s affect the successful outcome?

3. What service(s) do you give them?

Agencies must:

- Determine which customers are expected to receive which service(s) resulting in a specific outcome.
- Identify how many services are offered (count) and how often services are offered (frequency).
- Be able to recognize and assess the quality of the services offered.

It is important to determine the relationship between the service and the expected outcome. This is key in the evaluation of the effectiveness of the program in producing the desired results. Without this information, you cannot determine if the program should be expanded, reduced, or maintained.

Carter's Key Questions – Continued

6. What happens to the customers as a result of the service?

- Identify the outcome(s) to be achieved by the customer's participation in the service.

- Identify the number of customers who are projected to achieve the outcome and the number of customers who actually achieved the outcome.

- If there is only one service provided, it is easy to link it to an expected outcome or result. It is more difficult to assign or link expected outcomes where multiple services are provided.

  There are four possible relationships between provision of services and expected outcomes:
  - One Service: One Outcome
  - One Service: Multiple Outcomes
  - Multiple Services: One Outcome
  - Multiple Services: Multiple Outcomes

Note: Sometimes agencies provide services that are not expected to change lives. It is important to make the distinction about what is expected.

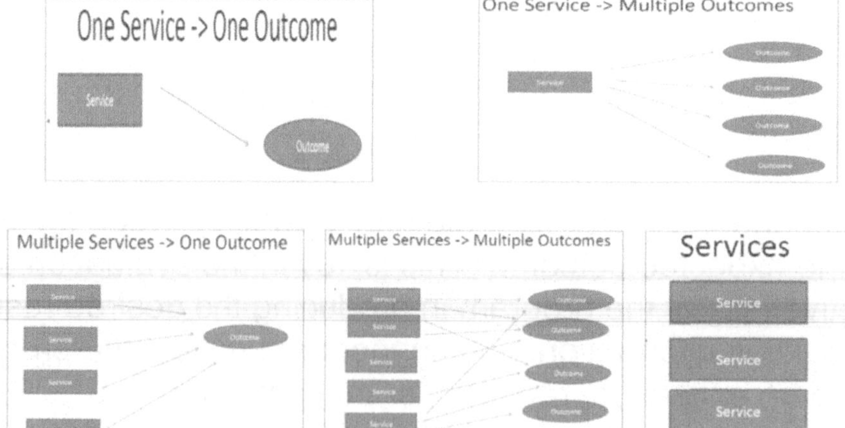

Characteristics of Outcome Indicators

In our Logic Model, outcomes are statements of results without numbers.

If we are to identify "what happens," we also need to be able to define the scope of the outcomes by establishing outcome indicators.

When you start adding numbers, you move from outcome statements to outcome indicator statements.

The outcome statement is a general statement of change without numbers. The outcome indicator is the statement of how much something has changed or how many have changed.

The indicator contains specific information about the scope of success. How many people changed? How much change was observed? How well was the outcome achieved?

Outcome Indicators meet all of these characteristics:

- Measurable.
- Simple, clear, and understandable.
- Realistic or attainable.
- Manageable.
- Identifies a specific customer or group of customers.
- Specifies a time frame.
- Measures an end, not a means to an end.

Some people refer to the mnemonic word, SMART, as a way to remember the elements of a good indicator — which covers most of the elements listed above:

- Specific (clear, understandable)
- Measurable
- Attainable (realistic)
- Relevant (to the specific customer or group)
- Time specific

Identifying Outcome Indicators

In the examples below, the outcome indicators identify what is observed and what can be measured to verify that a change was achieved.

Note: A clearly stated indicator will help you define what data will be collected as evidence that the outcome you expect has been achieved.

The outcome "school success" is too broad to allow you to measure it. You must decide what "indicates" school success. Some ideas are:

- Improved grades *(measured by a report card)*
- Reduced absences *(data also on report cards)*
- Improved behavior *(data collected from teacher observation)*

An indicator of "improved use of the English language" may include a specific improvement in the use of English, which could be measured -- for example by scores on the Basic English Skills Test (*BEST),* a standardized test used in English as a Second Language programs.

An indicator of "increased family functioning" may include specific behavior changes, which could be measured, for example, by scores on the Global Assessment Functioning Scale (GAF), *a standardized scale used in the mental health field that helps determine the level of functioning of an individual who is in care.*

Identifying the indicator requires even more specificity than what we have above. We need to quantify our expectations:

- How many students will improve?
- What is the expected improvement (by how much)?
- How many absences are acceptable?
- How will you quantify the improved behavior?

The indicator will include the number of customers who are expected to achieve the specifically defined "change" or outcome in relationship to the number who will receive service. It will also include a time frame.

Examples of Multiple Indicators for an Outcome

Example 1 – In some cases, the outcomes achieved by recipients of service may fall along a continuum.

The outcome of employment and training services to 50 customers is "obtaining a job." The primary indicator is:

- 10/50 customers obtain full-time jobs above minimum wage, including benefits, and are employed 90 days after placement.

Other indicators could include:

- 20/50 obtain permanent full-time jobs at minimum wage without benefits and are employed 90 days after placement
- 10/50 obtain part-time temporary jobs
- 5/50 obtain an "on-the-job training" opportunity
- 5/50 remain unemployed after 180 days in the program

Note: There are outcome indicators for all 50 customers.

Example 2 – In other cases (e.g., when referrals to other services may be involved), there may be multiple outcome indicators that cross a number of domains.

The outcome of providing case management services to 20 families could be "self-sufficiency." The range of indicators could include:

- 3/20 families increased their household income by 20% or more from all income sources;
- 1/20 persons opened a home-based childcare center (became self-employed);
- 5/20 families obtained safe, affordable rental housing;
- 1/20 families purchased a home;
- 3/20 persons achieved G.E.D. high-school equivalency diploma;
- 1/20 persons increased basic academic skills;
- 1/20 persons increased English language skills;
- 5/20 families continue to receive case management services but have not achieved any goal on their case management plan.

Note: In this example, each person achieved a different outcome, but in reality, one person could have achieved multiple outcomes.

National Indicators of Community Action Performance

As we have seen in Module One (History), the first mandated report of Community Action performance results was in 2001. The results reported between 2001 and 2003 were analyzed to produce a more standardized format to guide the reporting of community action outcomes.

From the 2003 NASCSP report:
"The Community Services Network is moving to balance the localized nature of its work and outcomes with the need to create a more uniform and accurate national accounting of how community action improves conditions and opportunities for low-income families and their communities.

"The National Performance Indicators are a selective sampling of what we do, and reflect only a portion of our work and accomplishments."
They reflect the most common outcomes achieved by Community Action.

"Because of the nature of the Community Services Block Grant, agencies participate in a broad range of activities to meet the unique needs of their communities. Each agency captures outcome data specific to its unique goals and priorities. It should be noted that not all agencies participate in the activities that generate outcomes for every national indicator, nor do these indicators represent all of the outcomes achieved by agencies."

"Guide to the National Indicators of Community Action Performance," NASCSP, 2004

As a part of the 2017 OMB Clearance process, a new set of NPIs was approved – the list of NPIs having been revised to reflect the current understanding of the work of Community Action across the country.
The NPIs are now organized by level rather than by Goal: Family NPIs are separated from Community NPIs.

Community Action Agencies are encouraged to continue to report annually on their full range of outcomes in addition to reporting on the required standard set of national indicators.
There are blank lines following the standard indicators where agencies are invited to include additional indicators.

Activity – Projected Family Level Outcome Indicators

Instructions: Consider the needs identified in Module 2 and the outcomes and strategies you identified in Module 3.

Now you will refine the outcomes to create a projected outcome indicator, including number to be served, number to achieve, and time frame.

Use this formula:

_______(a) out of ________(b) will achieve the outcome (as you plan to measure it) within this time frame: __________(c)

(a) Projection of the number of persons expected to achieve the outcome. This is the numerator.
(b) The total number of persons receiving the service. This is the denominator.
(c) The timeframe in which the outcomes will occur.

For example: 10 out of 50 persons in the employment program will obtain a job, six months after enrollment.

Note: In the Intro to ROMA training, we are building a family level logic model.

Family Level Logic Model

1	2	3	4	5	6	7	8
N	S	O	OI				
Mission:							

Module Four Review

1. Before you can implement the agency's strategic plan, you must consider what will be needed for quality service delivery. These include:

2. We use Reginald Carters Key Questions to help us understand the basic facts that must be available to us as we implement our plan. Please provide a brief explanation of the questions listed below:
   a. How many are you serving?

   b. Who are they?

   c. What services do you give them?

   d. What happens as a result of the service?

3. What are the four possible relationships between provision of services and expected outcomes?

4. What is the difference between an Outcome Statement and an Outcome Indicator?

5. What are the elements of a good indicator?

S	M	A	R	T

6. The National Performance Indicators are a standard set of indicators that are most commonly achieved by Community Action Agencies across the country. True or False

7. There are blank lines on the Annual Report to allow agencies to enter additional Indicators to supplement the standards ones provided. True or False

Module Five

Measuring Performance

Considering Standards

Key Points – Module Five:

- The Carter Questions can be used to identify performance and accountability.
- Customer Success Rates are a part of the complete outcome indicator.
- Baseball teaches us core principles of measuring performance.
- Industry standards for performance often support a low rate of success.
- Community Action Agencies can benefit from developing realistic performance standards for their programs.
- One agency success measure is the ability to predict (or target) outcome performance.

Using Carter's Seven Key Questions for Performance and Accountability

We identified the Carter Questions in Module 4 and showed how they could be used in planning and management. Now we need to think about using the data from these questions as a basis for calculating performance and establishing accountability measures at the family level.

The next addition to our logic model is a calculation that will produce a <u>measure of performance</u>.

In the creation of the indicator, we establish a relationship between the number of customers who were served and the number of customers who achieved results.
Such as: 10 out of 50 got a job.

This is the basis for the calculation that follows.

We will be identifying the <u>rate or percent of customer success</u> achieved as a result of a service.

Estimating Customer Performance

There are five steps used to estimate performance

1. **Identify the outcome(s).** This is a qualitative statement about what is going to be achieved, **with no numbers**. (Carter Question 6)

2. **Identify the service expected to produce the outcome.** (Carter Question 3)

3. **Identify the number of people receiving the service.** (Carter Question 1) Identify a timeframe as a part of the description of the service.

4. **Identify the outcome indicator(s).** This is a **quantitative statement** that includes the time frame for the achievement of the outcome.

5. **Estimate performance** by calculating the relationship between the number receiving the service and the number achieving the outcome. Divide the number expected to achieve the outcome (placed in the numerator of a fraction you are creating) by the number expected to receive the service (placed in the denominator of the fraction) to get a percent. This calculation yields a percentage: "projected success rate."

These steps occur prior to delivery of the service and are used to estimate customer performance expected to be the result of the service.

Example: A family self-sufficiency program has enrolled 20 families, in which each head of household is seeking employment as a Certified Nursing Assistant (CNA). These 20 individuals (D) will receive training over the next six months and support to seek employment. It is estimated or projected that 7 of the individuals (N) will become employed within six months of completing the training.

1. Outcome – Head of Household becomes employed as CNA.
2. Service/Activity– Family self-sufficiency program/Training for head of household.
3. Number to be served (D) – 20 individuals in a six-month period.
4. Outcome Indicator (N) – 7 individuals will become employed within six months of completing the training.
5. Projected Customer Success rate – 7 individuals who will achieve the outcome divided by 20 individuals who will receive services = 35% will succeed within the program year.

(N) 7 individuals will secure employment	= 35% **projected**
(D) 20 individuals will receive training	customer success rate

Measuring Actual Customer Performance

After the service, when you know what happened, you will determine your "actual success rate." The actual performance rate is calculated after delivery of the service using the same process as above but replacing the projected or targeted numbers with the actual numbers in both the numerator and the denominator.

- The program will identify the actual number of individuals who achieved the outcome and the number actually served, and will calculate the customer success rate. This requires follow-up, using identified measurement tools.
- **In the prior example:** A family self-sufficiency program has enrolled 20 families. The head of household seeking employment as a Certified Nursing Assistant, received training. After the program, the agency found the actual number to secure employment was 5 individuals.
- Five (5) individuals who achieved the outcome divided by 20 individuals who received services = 25% actually succeeded within the program year.

(N) 5 individuals secured employment (D) 20 individuals received training	= 25% **actual** customer success rate

Analysis of the Actual Results

If you are managing your program using results-oriented practices, you want to know how many individuals you need to serve to achieve certain goals. You will also want to know how attendance will impact the outcomes. Let's assume that some individuals who enroll will not complete the program. *("Enroll" means to actively start the program.)*

How do the "non-completers" affect your performance rate?

Measuring Actual Performance With a Reduced Denominator

In our example, the agency found that 5 of the 20 individuals who were originally enrolled in the training dropped out prior to completion. If 15 individuals completed the training, how does this affect the customer success rate?

Using the number of individuals who *completed the training* and became certified, we see a difference in the performance rate.

(N) 5 individuals secured employment	= 33% success rate for those
(D) 15 individuals *completed requirements*	who completed

It is useful to management to calculate both measures of performance for different reasons.
-- All people served must be identified to support the allocation of resources to the training.
-- Comparing the percent that represents all of the original enrollments (25% success), with the percent that represents those who completed the program (33% success), shows the positive difference in rate of success for the "completers." This is a measure of the effectiveness of the service.

Analysis of performance data will suggest different actions you may take to improve the number of customer successes. You may:

- Recruit and enroll larger numbers.
- Target specific individuals for the program, based on experience with successful customers.
- Modify the service delivery, based on follow up to identify barriers.

Reducing the Denominator When Fewer Were Actually Served

Another situation when you might use a reduced denominator is when the actual number of participants served was less than projected.

For example, if only 15 enrolled individuals actually received the training, and all of them completed and received certification, you would use the 15 as your denominator when calculating customer success.
Your analysis of this situation would include considering why the full number projected was not enrolled.

Activity – Customer Success Rate
An Addition to the Outcome Indicator

Instructions: Starting with the information you already identified for the Outcome Indicator, calculate the percent of customer success.

Projected Success Rate

________(a) out of ________(b) or ____________% (a/b) will (achieve the outcome) within the time frame: ___________(c)

(a) Projection of the number of persons expected to achieve the outcome. This is the numerator.
(b) Projection of the total number of persons to receive the service. This is the denominator.
(a/b) **Divide** the number who are expected to achieve the outcome by the number expected to receive the service. This is the projected customer success rate.
(c) The time frame (when the outcomes actually happened).

For example: 15 out of 20 persons in the employment program or 75% will obtain a job six months after enrollment.

Actual Success Rate

Once the service is complete, you will convert this statement by using (a) the number that *actually achieved*, (b) the number *actually served*, and the calculation of the actual customer success rate.

For example: 10 out of 20 persons in the employment program or 50% obtained a job six months after enrollment.

Family Level Logic Model

1	2	3	4	5	6	7	8
N	S	O	OI	R			

Mission:

Note: Amend the information you previously entered into the Outcome Indicator columns of the logic model by adding the percents.

How "good" is your customer success percent?
Is there a standard percent that is accepted for our work?

Performance Standards

How do you know what percent of success is realistic or achievable?

Activity – Let's Talk Baseball!

Instructions: You will receive a baseball card, which will be for a batter rather than a pitcher. On the back of the card is a batting average. Please write the batting average below. The batting average is a three-digit number beginning with a decimal point, e.g., .273. This is the statistic that is used to measure a batter's performance.

Write the batting average here:

Activity – Let's Talk Baseball! - Continued

In baseball, while we collect the number of times a player is "at bat," (attendance or participation), what baseball wants to know is the result, or outcome, of being "at bat." Did the player officially get up to bat and get a hit? This result <u>or outcome indicator</u> is a performance calculation called the batting average.

We can illustrate this with Yogi Berra's baseball card.

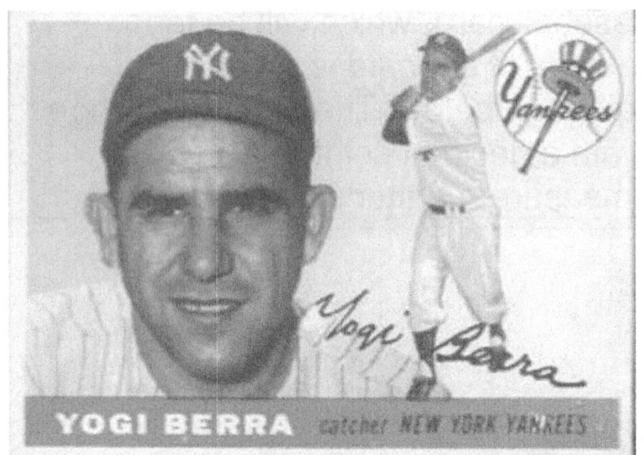

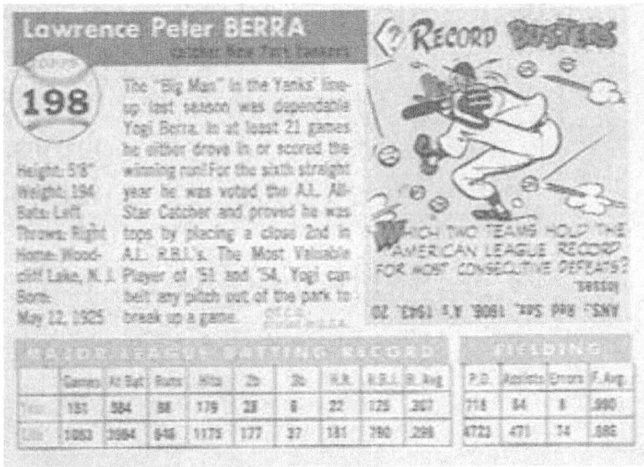

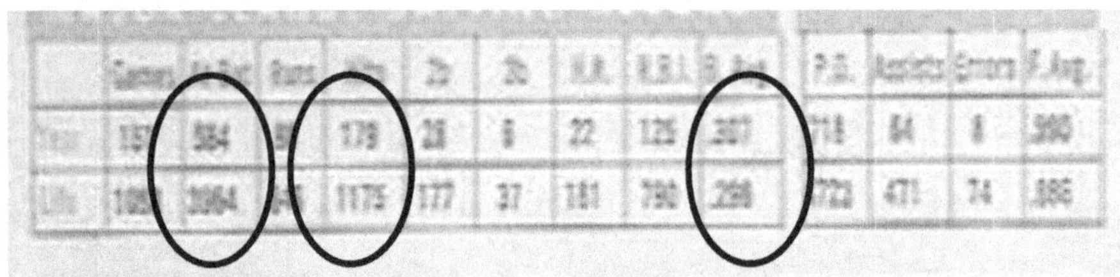

	Games	At Bat	Runs	Hits	2b	3b	H.R.	R.B.I.	B. Avg.	P.O.	Assists	Errors	F. Avg.
Year	151	584	88	179	28	6	22	125	.307	718	84	8	.990
Life	1063	3964	646	1175	177	37	181	790	.298	4723	471	74	.986

N = <u>179 hits</u> = .307 batting average
D = 584 times at bat

Yogi Berra successfully hit the ball and got on base 30.7% of the time. In baseball, a batting average:

- at .300 (30%) or greater is a superstar,
- between .299-.250 (29.9%-25%) is achieved by the majority of players,
- equal to or less than .249 (24.9%) is achieved by the least successful ball players.

Some know that Yogi Berra was a superstar, but unless baseball "taught" us that 30% was highly successful, by just looking at his statistics, we might have thought he was a failure.

What We Learn From Baseball

The first baseball statistics were collected, compiled into annual performance statistics and published by Henry Chadwick in 1859, 10 years before the start of organized baseball in 1869. In over 161 years, baseball has developed, analyzed and refined standards of performance based on the original work of Henry Chadwick.

Hitting .300, or succeeding about 30% of the time, is a recognized and accepted measure of excellence. The ball player who achieves this is a superstar. But if baseball had not discovered the relationship between the hitting standard and winning games, through the collection and analysis of data, we would not know that we are observing success at this level of performance.

What did baseball do that we don't do?

- Clearly defined the performance indicator (hit and get on base) related to the outcome (winning games)
- Observed performance and kept records
- Analyzed the data
- Developed a benchmark of excellence based on the analysis
- Publicized what they have learned (so that the public and other stakeholders know that 30% is excellent)

Continuous Improvement?

There has been little change in the definition of excellence over all the time that baseball has been keeping statistics. There have been many attempts to improve performance during that time. However, whether manufacturing better bats, designing and building ball parks to favor hitters, or changing the height of the pitching mound, nothing has increased the desirable performance rate of a baseball player: to hit above .300 on a regular basis.

Is it reasonable to expect a 10% improvement every year in our field?

Activity – Success Measures in Industry

References for Setting Public and Nonprofit Sector Expectations

- New Magazines: ____ % survive over 4 years.
- Movies: One in ___ or ____ % make a profit.
- Broadway Plays: One in ____ or _____ % make a profit.
- Prescription drugs: ____ % make it to market.
- Of the prescription drugs that make it to the market, ____ % make a profit.
- The survival rate of new business startups after four years is ______%
- Retail sales: One in ___ persons or ___% entering a store makes a purchase, compared to 2.3% on-line.
- On Time Railroad Delivery: + or - ____ hours.
- Baseball:
  - One hit in 3 times at bat (.333 or 33%) is a superstar.
  - One hit in 4 times at bat (.250 or 25%) is a successful hitter.

Community Action must establish its own standards of performance and communicate these standards of performance to elected officials, government, public and private funders, the general public, the media, and to the staff of CAAs and CSBG eligible entities.

Agency Ability to Target

In addition to the performance related to the number of outcomes achieved by the agency's customers compared to the number served, calculating the agency's ability to project (or target) their performance includes another dimension.

It is based on a different formula than the one we previously learned. The Outcome Indicator formula produces the measure of **customer success**. This is a measure of **agency success**.

Performance in this case refers back to one of the key provisions of GPRA: Agencies must be able to accurately identify performance goals or targets prior to beginning service. *(refer back to Module 1, p 4)*

"The ability of local CAAs to identify their own performance targets continues to be of interest to the Administration, to the Congress and to the national network of CAAs.

"The activity of engaging in successful targeting fulfills an essential need for compliance with elements of the Government Performance and Results Act (GPRA)."

NASCSP FY 2009 NPI Instruction Manual

In this performance calculation, you will be comparing the number of targeted or projected outcomes (which becomes the denominator), with the actual number who achieved those outcomes (which becomes the numerator).

This calculation does not use the number of those receiving services. This measurement compares two outcome data elements.

Your ability to manage your program(s) effectively depends on your ability to accurately project how many outcomes you expect to document. This success measure is designed to identify the ability of each CAA to project their performance.

Agency Targeting Success Rate

In the example used previously, we projected that 7 out of the 20 individuals who received training would achieve the outcome. This is the number projected – our target – and becomes the denominator of the fraction we are creating to establish the agency performance rate.

When the program was completed, we found that 5 individuals actually achieved the outcome. The actual number becomes the numerator of the fraction.

(N)	5 individuals secured employment (Actual) =	**71% targeting**
(D)	7 individuals projected to secure employment (Target)	**success rate**

Our ability to successfully project our performance for this project is 71%.

In the CSBG Annual Report, there is an auto-calculated "targeting column." It compares the reported number of outcomes projected and those outcomes reported as being actually achieved.

One reason why an agency might have under or over projected their outcomes:

If the number projected to be served is different from the number actually served, that will impact the agency's ability to achieve the number of outcomes that they projected.

Even though comparison of service numbers is not included in the CSBG Annual Report, it is information that is needed for the performance management and accountability of the agency.

It is important for the agency to have a process in place to consider the relationships among the projected and actual numbers served along with the numbers of those projected and actually achieving the outcome **as a standard part of any analysis of its own data.**

Can Success Rates Be More than 100%?

YES, the agency targeting ability success rate can be more than 100%.

Consider this alternate situation, in which 9 of the 20 individuals actually secured employment.

(N) 9 individuals secured employment (Actual)	=	**130% targeting**
(D) 7 individuals projected to secure employment (Target)		**success rate**

Is achieving 130% better than 71%? No, over performing is not better than underperforming when you are talking about targeting ability. Actually both of these results will require an explanation.

State CSBG offices that collect the data needed to compile the CSBG Annual Report, ask local agencies to provide follow-up explanations regarding any percent that is not within the 80% to 120% range.

Therefore, the example on the previous page would require a narrative because the targeting success rate was 71% and the example above (130%) would also be outside of the range.

We are using small numbers in this example, but if we multiplied by 10 or 100, the difference between the target number and the actual number becomes more apparent. If we projected 70 outcomes, the 80 -120 range for actual outcomes would be 56 to 84.

NO, the customer success rate can NOT be more than 100%.

In the indicator statements that we use to calculate customer success, the numerator is always less than, or equal to, the denominator. This is because you cannot have more people achieve an outcome than people who receive the service.

Module Five Review

1. What elements are compared to produce a Customer Success Rate?

2. Describe the difference between the Projected Customer Success Rate and the Actual Customer Success Rate:

3. Community Action has established standards of acceptable Customer Success Rates in all of the domains identified in the National Theory of change. True or False

4. Industry accepts a low percent of success when _______________

5. What did baseball do that the Community Action Network doesn't do?

6. What are the four elements of an Outcome Indicator?

7. The activity of engaging in successful targeting fulfills an essential need for compliance with elements of the Government Performance and Results Act (GPRA). True or False

8. The agency's ability to target (or project) the outcomes produced by their activities is calculated by comparing Projected Customer Success Rate and the Actual Customer Success Rate. True or False

9. An agency is considered to be effective in targeting if their success rate is over 100%. True or False

10. It is possible to have a Customer Success Rate over 100%. True or False

Module Six

Using Measurement Tools and Tracking Progress

Key Points – Module Six:

- Measurement tools and processes are needed to gather outcome and output data.
- An Outcome Scale describes different states or conditions of status and is used to identify and measure incremental change.
- Outcome Scales can be combined to form an Outcome Matrix to capture multiple interventions, needs, programs, and outcomes.
- Outcome Matrices may be modified to look at the relationships among different domains of well-being and social determinants of health.

Establishing Measurement Tools

Identifying the outcomes you expect to achieve includes considering how you will *measure* the accomplishments or outcomes that are the result of your outputs or services. The discussion about the outcome indicator in the previous module provided the calculations related to rates of success, and now this discussion is about how you will measure the indicator and prove what happened.

A data collection or measurement tool must be able to capture data for each program or service – quantifying both the outputs and the outcomes.

A Few Examples of OUTPUT Measurement Tools:

- Intake forms/screens
- Initial assessment forms
- Attendance logs
- Agency payment or expenditure records

A Few Examples of OUTCOME Measurement Tools

- Pre- and post-test.
- Customer financial records
- Employment records
- School reports
- Observation logs

Data Quality

The data secured from the measurement tools must be guided by clear policies, procedures and processes that assure the quality of the data. Data quality has four dimensions:

- Complete. There is no information missing from the data.
- Accurate. There are no mistakes in the data; all of the data elements are correct.
- Timely. The data is collected on time, on a regular basis, and/or is recent enough to be pertinent.
- Reliable. The data collected is meaningful to the topic. It is collected the same way every time, and the people involved in collecting data understand what they are responsible for collecting.

Identifying Evidence

Drucker reminded us, that as we have looked at qualitative and quantitative data related to identification of need, we must also identify both qualitative and quantitative measures of outcomes and outputs.

> "Progress and achievement can be appraised in *qualitative* and *quantitative* terms. These two types of measures are interwoven – they shed light on one another – and both are necessary to illuminate in what ways and to what extent lives are being changed."
>
> - "Qualitative measures address the depth and breadth of change within a particular context. Qualitative results can be in the realm of the intangible, such as instilling hope in a patient battling cancer.... Qualitative data, although sometimes more subjective and difficult to grasp, are just as real, just as important, and can be gathered just as systematically as the quantitative."
> - "Quantitative measures use defined standards. Quantitative appraisal offers valid hard data. Quantitative measures are essential for assessing whether resources are properly concentrated for results, whether progress is being made, whether lives and communities are changing for the better."
>
> *Drucker: What are Our Results? Question Four*

We must have a clear idea about the types of measurement tools that are most appropriate for the outcomes we will measure.

Think about the question: "How do you know?"

- What proof can you provide that an outcome has been achieved?
- What documentation do you have?
- How do you know that it is related to the service (output) provided?

As you are selecting the measurement tools, be sure to identify processes:

- Who will be responsible for data collection and storage of the data? How is the collection and storage done?
- Who reviews the data and how frequently is it reviewed?
- How often is data collected? How often reported? Who receives the reports? What happens to the data once it is reported?

Note: "storage" can refer to an electronic data base or other method of holding the collected data. The data base is not itself the measurement tool but is where the data is kept and aggregated.

Consider When to Use Soft Outcomes

Occasionally, agencies identify outcomes that are called "soft" outcomes because there is little "hard data" available to support these outcomes. Soft outcomes are usually verified by using subjective, qualitative data. Examples of "soft" outcomes include:

- Achievement of self-esteem (or self-confidence or other quality-of -life). This is acceptable if it is part of an overall comprehensive assessment measuring other types of functioning as well.

- Meeting or exceeding one's own goals. This is sometimes identified as an outcome without identifying the goals. If you have a population who all have different goals, putting them together in this kind of "catch all" statement can diminish the value of the individual outcomes, without an easy way to disaggregate them.

The agency must recognize some cautions about using qualitative data:

- Self-report of achieving an outcome, without any objective backup, may have limited value if there is question about the validity of the reporting process. It is difficult to standardize this data, so it should not be the only measure of customer success.

- Use of customer satisfaction surveys. It is important for customers to "like" the service, of course, but this cannot be the only measure of program success. How and to whom the survey is distributed and the number of respondents also affects the usefulness of the data. Also the timing of the survey can impact results and may not provide an accurate representation of experience. For instance, responses in January may be focused on heating issues while response in June may focus on summer programs.

- Anecdotal stories can be very effective if they are part of a report that also has other data. If they are the only measure of success, they may not be representative of the full range of your customers. Remember that stories and data should go together.

A Couple of Shortcuts

Use a Preexisting Measurement Tool

There are existing tools that may be available for measuring outcomes. CAAs should be encouraged to use these existing outcome measurement tools before creating their own.

Examples:

- Education programs, such as Adult Basic Education (ABE) and English as a Second Language (ESL), have standardized outcome measurement tools available.
- Counseling and behavior modification programs also have tools to measure changes in function such as the Global Assessment of Functioning Scale (GAF).
- Standardized measures of success in employment and training programs include statistics from Department of Labor and local labor markets.

Research Other Organizations That Have an Outcome Framework

There are many organizations with national affiliations that have made significant investments in their own outcome evaluation and reporting systems. Rather than duplicate work, efforts should be made to include the same outcomes and measures that these organizations report to their regional affiliates or national headquarters.

Organizations believed to have national outcome evaluation and reporting requirements include: American Red Cross, Big Brothers Big Sisters, Boys and Girls Clubs, Girl Scouts, Salvation Army, United Way, YMCA, YWCA, and other service organizations.

Faith-based organizations such as Catholic Social Services, Lutheran Services, and Jewish Family Service may also use standardized measurement tools.

Government agencies such as HUD also have standardized measures that could be referenced.

Activity – Family Level Measurement Tools and Processes

<u>Instructions:</u> Consider the needs, outcomes, services and indicators you previously identified. First identify what is needed to document the outputs. Then identify what is needed to document the outcomes?

What measurement tools will you use to document your **outputs?**	Who will be responsible? How will the data be collected?	What is the frequency of data collection and reporting?

What measurement tools will you use to document your **outcomes/results**?	Who will be responsible? How will the data be collected?	What is the frequency of data collection and reporting?

Note: In the Intro to ROMA training, we are building a family level logic model.

Family Level Logic Model

1	2	3	4	5	6	7	8
N	S	O	OI		M	D	F
Mission:							

Introduction to Outcome Scales

An Outcome Scale is a continuum that describes different states or conditions of status and is used to identify and measure incremental change in families, agencies and communities.

An automobile gas gauge is one example of a very simple scale.

Without having the definitions of the labels on the gauge (F, ¾, ½, ¼, E), we can recognize a continuum ranging from most desirable status (Full), to least desirable status (Empty). We "monitor" the gas gauge because it shows the changing amount of gas in the tank as we travel, indicated by placement on the scale.

The Outcome Scale methodology used in Community Action is a five-point continuum of outcome benchmarks that can be used to identify different states or conditions of status ranging from Thriving to In-Crisis, not unlike the continuum presented by the gas gauge. The scale methodology originally developed in the early 1990s by the CSBG Monitoring and Assessment Task Force (MATF) does not provide definitions for the five scale benchmarks. Rather, it was the intent of the MATF, that definitions would be developed by local consensus where specific outcomes would be associated with one of the five benchmarks on a scale in a given domain*.

Gas Gauge	MATF Scale
F	Thriving
¾	Safe
½	Stable
¼	Vulnerable
E	In-Crisis

**Early work in creating samples of definitions associated with scale benchmarks was done by Frederick Richmond. The Family Self Sufficiency Scale was developed in 1995 by Richmond working with the Bucks County Opportunity Council in Doylestown, PA. The MATF "Scales and Ladders" Committee and others throughout the country (such as the IL Association of Community Action Agencies) also worked on providing local agencies with sample scales beginning at that time. There are many current examples of scales in use throughout the country.*

Considering Intervention

The “Prevention Line” was added to distinguish between levels of independence or self-sufficiency.

Gas Gauge	MATF Scale
F	Thriving
3/4	Safe
1/2	Stable
Prevention Line	
1/4	Vulnerable
E	In-Crisis

Placement on a benchmark above the Prevention Line is considered a measure of independence, and placement on a benchmark below the Prevention Line is an indication of dependence or need for intervention.

The Prevention Line is a trigger for intervention. Consider when you would stop to add gas to your tank. The closer you move toward E, the more likely it is that the intervention needed will be more difficult and more costly.

The same is true with interventions provided by the Community Action network. It is easier to move to self-sufficiency if you are in a stable situation. Being vulnerable or in-crisis will present additional barriers for progress.

In Community Action, Outcome Scales are used to track incremental change between the scale benchmarks which allow us to “document” the movement from conditions of dependency to increasing self-sufficiency.

The graphic representation of the Outcome Scale makes it an effective tool to help visualize this progress.

Benefits of Outcome Scales

Outcome Scales have been recognized by many disciplines in the health and social services fields when it is important to measure functioning and incremental change.

For example, Outcome Scales have been used in the mental health field to determine when it is appropriate to move a patient from a more to a less restrictive setting, or to discharge from a hospital back into the community.

The data collected and analyzed from placement on an outcome scale supports the management of the customer/client and improves decision-making.

Outcome Scales can be used to:

- help visualize the “big picture” of the situation facing the customer at the initial meeting by reviewing the range of conditions on the scale;
- measure change by comparing scale placement at two or more different times indicating positive, negative, or no change (characterized as neutral or stable);
- determine how much progress and the time it takes an individual to reach the next scale benchmark;
- capture incremental change, interim success, and progress towards long-term goals as interim goals are achieved;
- identify areas where progress has not been made towards achieving long-term goals - for the purpose of identifying both barriers and potential solutions;
- recognize any movement in a positive direction on the outcome scale as movement toward self-sufficiency (such as movement from “In-Crisis” to “Vulnerable”); and
- support development of a case management plan where goals for movement towards stability and self-sufficiency are established.

Activity-Part One
Developing a Family Level Housing Outcome Scale

Instructions

Think about all the various types and conditions of housing available in your community. Write down the possibilities here.

Consider both best and worst-case scenarios.

Activity-Part Two
Developing a Housing Outcome Scale

Instructions: In the template below, begin by transferring the housing conditions from the previous page to the benchmark that best describes the condition until all housing conditions are transferred.

Hint: It is often helpful to view the top end of the scale as the "best" case scenario and the lowest end of the scale as the "worst" case scenario.

Benchmarks	Family Level Housing Conditions
Thriving	Private Homeownership
Safe	Student Housing, Elderly, Permanent Supportive Housing
Stable	Trailer Park, Section 8
	Prevention Line
Vulnerable	Temporary Housing
In-Crisis	Shelter

Stop!! Stop!! Stop!!

The next page contains a sample Housing Outcome Scale which should only be reviewed after you have completed this activity.

Sample Housing Scale

Outcome Level ☑ Family ☐ Agency ☐ Community

Benchmarks	Outcomes
Thriving (9-10) **Independent**	**Housing of Choice – Non-Subsidized** Safe and secure non-subsidized home ownership of choice (House, Condominium, Co-Op). (10A) Safe and secure non-subsidized rental housing of choice. (10B)
Safe (7-8) **Independent**	**Limited Choice of Housing – Non-Subsidized** Safe and secure non-subsidized home ownership; limited choices due to moderate income. (8A) Safe and secure non-subsidized rental housing; limited choices due to moderate income. (8B)
Stable (5-6) (May include elements of dependency) **Independent**	**Limited Choice of Housing – Subsidized** Safe and secure Section 8 housing. (6A) Safe and secure subsidized rental apartment. (6B) Safe and secure public housing. (6C) Safe and secure permanent living arrangements with others. (5)
	Prevention Line
Vulnerable (3-4) **Dependent**	**Temporary Housing or At-Risk of Losing Housing** Safe and secure transitional housing (30 to 60 days). (4A) Living with others – temporary arrangements. (4B) Unaffordable home ownership or rental. (3)
In-Crisis (0-2) **Dependent**	**Imminent Loss of Housing Pending, Short-term, Unsafe or No Housing** Safe shelter (up to 30 days). (2A) Notice of mortgage foreclosure. (2B) Notice of eviction from rental apartment or rental house. (2C) Unsafe Shelter. (1A) Substandard or unsafe ownership or rental. (1B)
	Homelessness. (0)

Please note: This is one example and not suggested to be the "right" (or only) Housing Scale. It reflects the housing conditions in a specific community and is based on local consensus.

Analysis of the Sample Housing Scale

The type of Outcome Scale you create may be different from other communities. In all likelihood, it will take negotiators within the group to identify the conditions (outcomes) and where to associate them to the scale benchmarks.

For example, public housing could be associated with any of the five scale benchmarks depending on the location, quality of housing, and conditions in the neighborhood. Outcome statements are written to approximate actual conditions, and their placement on an outcome scale must be accepted by all who use the scale.

- Some Outcome Scales include headers in each benchmark to help decide where to place the outcomes. Such as “Limited Choice” or “Unsafe.”

- When a benchmark contains more than one outcome, there are two possible situations: either the outcome conditions or statements can have the same value (e.g., conditions in Stable are considered equal: 6A, 6B, 6C) or different values (e.g., In-Crisis conditions are unequal within the same benchmark: 2A, 2B, 2C,1A,1B, 0).

Only one outcome condition is placed in each scale benchmark unless assigned an individual score as described above.

- Numbers provide a shortcut to understanding placement on an Outcome Scale within benchmarks.

- In this model, a score of five (5) or greater is placement above the Prevention Line indicating benchmarks of independence or self-sufficiency, while a score below five (5) or lower indicates benchmarks of dependence.

Administering an Outcome Scale

Measuring movement on a scale will be inaccurate if the initial placement is faulty. You must have a reliable way to establish the baseline.

It is important to establish a standardized procedure for placement on an Outcome Scale. Once the benchmark definitions are agreed upon, everyone who administers the scale must use the same process and established definitions for each benchmark. Any interview, assessment, and subsequent placement on an Outcome Scale, must be done in an objective manner.

One way to administer an outcome scale is to present the scale conditions or outcome statements without the scale benchmarks or numbers to the customer - as that may bias their response. The individual being assessed is asked to choose the one statement that best reflects their present condition or situation. The first or initial assessment is documented as the baseline or need for service.

This is an example of statements related to the housing domain.

Safe and secure non-subsidized home ownership or rental housing of choice
Safe and secure non-subsidized home ownership or rental housing – with choices limited due to moderate income.
Safe and secure Section 8 housing.
Safe and secure subsidized rental apartment.
Safe and secure public housing.
Safe and secure permanent living arrangements with others.
Safe and secure transitional housing (30-60 days).
Living with others – temporary arrangements.
Unaffordable home ownership or rental.
Safe shelter (up to 30 days).
In danger of loss of housing (e.g., notice of mortgage foreclosure or eviction from rental unit).
Unsafe Shelter.
Substandard or unsafe ownership or rental.
Homelessness.

Note: This process is typically based on the customer's perspective, and not on necessarily on evidence provided. It is good practice to have the ability to go back and adjust the intake information if additional data are acquired that would challenge the original placement.

Documenting Placement on an Outcome Scale

As customer progress is observed, it is essential to document any movement both within and across the scale benchmarks. Each benchmark on the scale has associated outcomes.

While the Outcome Scale is a tool to *track progress*, you will need to gather the data from an appropriate measurement tool to support placement on the scale.

In the beginning of this module, we identified output and outcome measurement tools. Remember that you will have to gather data from a reliable source so that you can mark the benchmark on the scale accurately.

Some agencies have created a survey using the language of the Scale's Benchmarks, and that survey becomes the measurement tool that is administered to the customer periodically throughout service or at follow up intervals.

The survey is a tool used to get customer report about their status.

> Of course, sometimes customers will rate their own status higher (or lower) than it actually is. Agency staff must have ways to understand and work with this phenomenon.

Consider: If progress is based on customer reporting (which is their own perspective), what other evidence or documentation would be useful to verify progress? Is additional evidence is needed?

Some intake assessments include eligibility documentation that would be a guide for placement on an "income" scale. Placement on the scale should be consistent with what is entered in the intake record, considering family size, etc. Staff should check to see that the data they are entering into the scale matches the data collected from intake.

Reporting Using an Outcome Scale

When the initial or baseline assessment and placement on an Outcome Scale is compared to additional assessments over time, the comparison of these placements yields three possibilities: a positive change, negative change, or no change.

The movement from one outcome to another (between or within outcome benchmarks) is documented and reported.

It is also important to document and report where there is no change.

The individual benchmarks, or outcomes identified within the benchmarks on the Outcome Scale, are the reportable outcomes, not the labels "Thriving" to "In-Crisis."

It is not appropriate to report that the customer "moved up" one benchmark on the outcome scale since movement from one benchmark to another will mean different things to each agency. Even when multiple agencies are using the same outcome scales, it is the actual outcome that is documented and reported.

In the Housing example, you would not report that the person moved up two benchmarks from In-Crisis to Safe. You would report that the person acquired permanent "Safe and secure non-subsidized housing," which is a measurable outcome.

Introduction to the Outcome Matrix

As we have seen, the Outcome Scale helps measure incremental change in a single category or domain. Think of the previous example of a Housing Scale.

In the human condition, we know "well-being" or achieving a level of self-sufficiency depends on the congruence of multiple factors that allows us to be functional on a daily basis.

In general, we accept the need for families to have a wage earner with sufficient income to meet the expenses of the household – to provide for good housing, food, transportation, childcare (if needed), discretionary spending, etc. If each of these was on a separate Outcome Scale, we would want them to all be above the Prevention Line to identify independence.

When we select a number of scales that most relate to the overall circumstance that we are interested in measuring, we create an Outcome Matrix.

At its simplest, an Outcome Matrix is a grouping of Outcome Scales arranged side by side.

The choice of the various Outcome Scales that comprise an Outcome Matrix will affect the data you collect and analyze and the story you wish to tell. For example, an "employment" program may want to include scales related to education, childcare, and transportation. A "parent education" program may want to include scales related to parent/child interaction, food and nutrition, and health. A "case management" program may select scales related to income, housing, financial literacy, and asset development.

Note: Bill Hamilton, Community Action Marin, San Rafael, CA, was an early developer of the matrix concept. He produced matrices in all three levels (family, agency, and community) in 1995, which were used as an aid to planning. The focus of the matrix to include outcomes at each benchmark and the labels on the rows and columns were adapted by Richmond for use in the Bucks County Family Self Sufficiency Matrix in 1995 and for ongoing implementation of ROMA.

Sample Family Outcome Matrix --
1st Assessment–Feb. 1, 2nd Assessment–May 1, 3rd Assessment–Aug. 1

In each domain, the status of the family is indicated by the date that is in the box below the statement.

Domains / Benchmarks	Income	Employment	Housing	Education and Training	Transportation	Childcare
Thriving (9-10)	> 200% of poverty adjusted for family size.	Full-time work above minimum wage with employer-provided benefits.	Home Ownership Condominium Ownership Co-Op Home Ownership Non-subsidized rental housing	Post-Secondary degree: Masters or doctorate. Post-Secondary degree: bachelors, associates.	Family members always have transportation needs met through public transportation, a car, or a regular ride.	Child enrolled in unsubsidized, licensed childcare setting of own choice.
Safe (8-9)	Between 176%-200% of poverty adjusted for family size.	Full-time work above minimum wage without employer-provided benefits.	Safe and secure non-subsidized housing, <u>choices</u> <u>limited</u> due to moderate income,	Post high school vocational education, non college business, <u>or</u> technical <u>or</u> vocational training, <u>or</u> some college credits	**Family members have most transportation needs met through public transportation, a car, or a regular ride.**	Child enrolled in licensed, subsidized childcare
		Aug 1			Aug. 1	May 1 Aug 1
Stable (5-6)	Between 126%-175% of poverty adjusted for family size.	Full-time work at minimum wage without employer- provided benefits.	Safe and secure <u>subsidized</u> rental apartment.	High school diploma or G.E.D.	**Family members have some transportation needs met through public transportation, a car, or a regular ride.**	Child provided childcare by a family member or friend. Child provided childcare by various caregivers
	Aug. 1	May 1	Aug 1	Feb. 1 May 1 Aug 1	May 1	
	Prevention Line		Prevention Line		Prevention Line	
Vulnerable (3-4)	Between 100%-125% of poverty adjusted for family size.	Part-time employment	Safe and secure transitional housing	Reading, writing, and basic math skills present, no high school diploma or G.E.D.	Family members have few transportation needs met.	Child on waiting list for enrollment in childcare.
	May 1	Feb 1	Feb. 1 May 1		Feb. 1	Feb. 1
In-Crisis (0-2)	Between 50%-100% of poverty (by family size.)	Unemployed	Living with relatives Substandard or unsafe Homeless	Reading, writing, and basic math skills absent.	Family members do not have public transportation, a car, or regular ride	Child not enrolled in childcare.)
	Feb. 1					

Sample Family Outcome Matrix Activity

In the Outcome Matrix presented on the prior page, you will find six areas an agency selected to use to define the "well-being" of a family.

- Income
- Employment
- Housing
- Education and Training
- Transportation
- Childcare

This sample shows the placement of a family on the matrix at three time periods. The status at the time of placement is indicated below the box.

Instructions: Please take five minutes to analyze the family outcome matrix by yourself. Identify at least four changes that have occurred in the status of the family. After you have analyzed the matrix, participate in a small group discussion and prepare an overall assessment of the changes that have taken place since the initial intake on February 1st.

Income:

Employment:

Housing:

Education:

Transportation:

Childcare:

Overall Assessment:

Social Determinants of Health

A specific kind of family Outcome Matrix can be configured with outcome scales in various domains that are identified as being social determinants of health.

"Social Determinants of Health (SDOH) are conditions in the environments in which people are born, live, learn, work, play, worship, and age that affect a wide range of health, functioning, and quality-of-life outcomes and risks."

A matrix that includes elements which are involved in social determinants of health will provide the "big picture" regarding what is affecting the individual or family well-being. Addressing and resolving fundamental well-being risk factors, is a necessary first step for the customer to achieve stability and move towards self-sufficiency.

When using a matrix like this, the initial or baseline assessment will identify the emergent and/or urgent health risk factors placed below the Prevention Line.

Social and Health Determinants of Poverty

More than 80 percent of a person's health is tied to factors other than clinical care including availability of or access to nutritious food, health care, safe and affordable housing, education opportunities for all ages, reliable transportation, and community supports.

Having access to resources, or experiencing a lack of access to these resources, can have a significant influence on population health outcomes and are related to conditions of poverty.

When the determinants of health work against someone or are left unaddressed, they create health inequalities — which lead to worse outcomes and more expensive care. These underlying drivers of health impact every part of our physical, mental, and social well-being.

There is a relationship between health and economic status. One impacts the other.

Poor health can be the result of poverty, and poverty can be the result of poor health.

Poverty undermines a wide range of human capabilities, potential, and opportunities. Child hunger and poor health are barriers to school success and, therefore, lead to a later inability to find good work as an adult, limiting ability to support a family. Thus, the downward spiral that maintains poverty continues.

For more information:
https://www.amerihealthcaritas.com/beyond-managed-care/social-determinants-health.aspx?gclid=CjwKCAiAgqDxBRBTEiwA59eEN_Ja45xaTilKo5NjuMn7W5xi2zJ9ZIvVt3_titeG5OdmbKUOmIJWoRoCjFYQAvD_BwE

Characteristics of the Outcome Matrix

As with the individual Outcome Scales found within the Matrix, the initial, or baseline assessment, and placement is compared to additional assessments conducted over time to identify progress.

By using a common framework, outcome scales combined into an outcome matrix can be aggregated and provide a multidimensional look at the agency's work to show movement in multiple domains.

Aggregation is important because it allows agencies to present data on a number of both customers and programs in a uniform and quantifiable manner.

An outcome matrix is used to:

- capture progress (incremental change) of a single customer or group of customers across more than one scale (program or service) and over time;
- capture agency data across multiple programs and services;
- identify areas of strengths (above the prevention line) and where improvement is needed (below the prevention line);
- identify the relationship between different domains of a problem or where outcome scales interrelate;
- create a mini-needs assessment based on the "experience" of the population being tracked;
- consider adjustment of agency resource allocation to areas where it will be the most efficient and effective.

Note: The sample matrix in this module is at the family level. Matrices at the agency and community levels have the same functions but are designed for a different focus.

See www.roma-nptp.org for samples of community and agency matrices.

Module Six Review

1. The agency must identify measurement tools to be able to capture data for each program or service, quantifying both the outputs and the outcomes. True or False

2. Identify the dimensions required to assure data quality (circle all that apply):

Accurate	Complete	Contemporary
Reliable	Resource-based	Timely

3. An example of a “soft” outcome is:

4. What is the limitation of using soft outcomes?

5. An Outcome Scale describes different states or conditions of status and is used to identify and measure incremental change. True or False

6. Even without a reliable method for baseline placement, tracking movement on an Outcome Scale is valid. True or False

7. Placement on a scale is done differently by all staff that use the scale, depending on their own program guidelines. True or False

8. An Outcome Matrix is: ______________________________

9. Outcome Matrices always have the same domains, regardless of the program for which it is being used. True or False.

10. There is a relationship between health and economic status: one impacts the other. True or False

Module Seven

Managing Performance with the Logic Model

Key Points – Module Seven:

- A logic model is like a story with a connecting narrative, so the data entered in all eight columns must match or be connected to the other columns.
- A logic model can include short, intermediate, and long-term outcomes.
- While each has a unique function, logic models and scales can be used together to analyze data for improved program management and decision-making.
- Community Action Agencies can use logic models in many ways: to check the relationships of their planned interventions and outcomes, to communicate with funders and other key stakeholders, to track progress towards goals, and to improve decision-making.

Understanding the Logic Model

The logic model is used to support planning, monitoring, evaluation, and other management and accountability functions of the agency. It is a ROMA tool that links program operations, and program accountability.

In the ROMA Logic Model:

Program operations, in Columns 1-5 include:

- Need-Problem or Situation--Column 1
- Intervention-Service or Activity--Column 2
- Outcome--Column 3
- Projected Outcome Indicator--Column 4
- Actual Outcome Indicator--Column 5

Program accountability in Columns 6-8 of the logic model include:

- Measurement Tools--Column 6
- Data Procedures--Column 7
- Frequency of Data Collection, Reporting and Analysis--Column 8

The agency or program mission statement is found across the bottom of the ROMA Logic Model, indicating its place as the foundation on which the other information is built.

We have been "building" a logic model throughout Modules 1-6. This has allowed us to identify principles and practices behind each of the eight columns.

We will now look at the ROMA Logic Model as a whole, to make sure the data entered in all eight columns "matches" (e.g., that each column is connected or associated with each other column). Think of the ROMA Logic Model as a story with a connecting narrative.
(A handout will be provided for this activity)

Activity-Does the Information Match?

Instructions

The information in the columns of the Logic Model must "match." The elements must be connected in realistic and appropriate ways. You will be given sample information to review and discuss.

Decide if:

- the need is clearly stated;
- the identified outcome meets the stated need;
- the intervention or service will produce the outcome;
- the outcome indicator relates directly to the outcome and can be measured;
- the measurement tools will produce evidence; and,
- appropriate personnel and procedures are identified.

Activity
Building a Family Level Logic Model
Part One

Program Management

There is a blank logic model provided to do this activity. We have added another blank in the Appendix for future use. If you use this logic model template in your work, please keep the footer intact.

Instructions:
You will be creating a Family Level Logic Model in this activity.

- If you were doing this "in real life" you would have already identified need/s (from the Community Needs Assessment process). You would have identified outcome/s and services related to the need (from your planning processes).
- Think of this activity as if you are "transferring" your previous work to a graphic presentation.
- Begin building your logic model by considering a program that you know that provides direct services to individuals and families. Identify the program name and the program mission statement. Enter these on the logic model template.

Starting on the left side of the logic model template:

Identify the need in Column 1.
Create outcome language for Column 3.
Identify, in Column 2, the specific intervention/service.
Identify outcome indicators that will demonstrate that the outcome has been achieved and enter Column 4.

Notes:

- Do not use a program that has a proxy outcome in this activity.
- Identify a spokesperson to present your group work to the other participants.

Activity
Building a Family Level Logic Model
Part Two

Measuring and Documenting Results

Instructions: Using the work just completed for Columns 1-4, decide how you will collect and store data to measure, document, and report on your program. You will be completing Columns 6, 7, and 8.

Identify the Measurement Tools, which are used to collect the raw data about outputs and outcomes and enter them in Column 6.

Identify the, Data Procedures and the Personnel Needed for Data Collection, Storage and Analysis, and enter this in Column 7.
The collection procedures will describe the method(s) for gathering data during implementation of the service using the tools identified in column 6 and any other processes necessary to secure documentation (proof) of both outputs and outcomes. Storage refers to the place where data are maintained, e.g., individual case records, central database, a specialized database. It can also refer to the actual location, e.g., on-site, with a subcontractor, or online. Storage may be accessed manually or electronically to use in reporting and analysis of the data. Procedures must include the personnel assigned to the tasks of collection, storage, retrieval and analysis of data.

Identify the Frequency of Data Collection, Reporting and Analysis. This refers to how often data are collected, and how often data is reported. Also identify when (how frequently) the data is analyzed. These time frames may be based on requirements or on program needs. Enter in Column 8.

Identify a spokesperson to present your group work on Columns 6, 7, and 8 to the other participants.

Note: Why have we skipped Column Five? *That is the Actual Results Column, which is completed after the service is provided and the data are collected.*

ROMA Logic Model

National ROMA Peer-To-Peer Training Program

Organization: **Program:** ☐ **Family**

Need **Problem, Situation**	**Intervention** **Service or Activity** Identify the # of customers to be served and the time frame for the project. *May also include the # of units of service offered.*	**Outcome** General statement of results expected without numbers	**Projected Outcome Indicator** # of customers expected to achieve each outcome divided by the number expected to be served; projected % of customer success	**Actual Outcome Indicator** # of customers actually achieving the outcome, divided by the number actually served; actual % of customer success	**Measurement Tools** What evidence will you collect to prove your outputs were delivered and outcomes were achieved?	**Data Procedures** Include Collection, Storage and Analysis Procedure; Personnel Responsible	**Frequency** **of Data Collection, Reporting and Analysis**
(1) Planning	**(2) Intervention**	**(3) Benefit**	**(4) Performance**	**(5) Performance**	**(6) Accountability**	**(7) Accountability**	**(8) Accountability**
Mission:							

Family Level Logic Model Checklist

- ❑ Was the Mission of the organization or program identified? (Foundation)
- ❑ Is the Need statement clear? (not a "need for a service" but the identification of what is needed or lacking) (Column 1)
- ❑ Does the Intervention *match* the Need? (Columns 1-2)
- ❑ Does the Intervention include the number to be served and the time frame? Is the time frame realistic? (Column 2)
- ❑ Does the Outcome (Column 3) match the Need (Column 1)? Can the Outcome result from the identified Intervention (Column 2)? Is it a statement without numbers?
- ❑ Is the Outcome realistic, clear, and attainable? (Column 3) *(Does the Outcome avoid words like "received" which makes the statement appear to relate only to the receipt of a service and not an outcome – rather does it say what will change?)*
- ❑ Does the Projected Outcome Indicator provide a way to measure the Outcome? Are the Outcome Indicators realistic, clear, and attainable? (Column 4)
- ❑ Does the Projected Outcome Indicator include the number expected to achieve the outcome, number to be served, the percent that represents the relationship between these two numbers (projected % of customer success) and a time frame? (Column 4)
- ❑ If this is a logic model created after services have been delivered, identify the Actual Outcome Indicator, including actual numbers who achieved, actual number who were served, the percent that represents the relationship between the actual numbers (actual % of customer success), and the time frame (Column 5)
- ❑ Were specific Measurement Tools identified? Were both output and outcome measurement tools identified? (Column 6)
- ❑ Are the data collection and storage procedures and personnel specific? (Column 7)
- ❑ Is the frequency of data collection sufficient to support monitoring progress and outcomes? Are the intervals of reporting clearly identified? Is there a time frame for analysis of the data? (Column 8)

Analysis guidance:
Are the actual results consistent with the projected numbers? What is the agency's ability to target its performance? This is the percent that represents the relationship between the number who actually achieved and the number projected to achieve.

Using the Logic Model to Analyze Program Data

In the logic model on the next page, Emergency Housing 1.0, the agency's mission is: To ensure that all families have safe, clean shelter.
(This logic model is based on an actual situation at a local CAA.)

Column 1 documents two specific needs: "Families are at risk of being evicted" and "Families are homeless." These are two distinct needs.

Two services/interventions are provided:

- One month emergency rent payment
- Emergency shelter placement.

The assumptions behind the program are that issuance of a rent check or admittance to the shelter, automatically assures 30 days of safe shelter.

The agency projected it would serve 200 families, of which150 would receive emergency rent payment and 50 would receive emergency shelter placement. It projected that 100% of these families would achieve 30 days of stability.

Follow up was done at the Emergency Shelter at 30 days and data entered into Column 5. An analysis of the data indicates that the emergency shelter service is operating as expected.

Follow up data for the emergency rent payment service was collected after 30, 60 and 90 days and entered into Column 5. An analysis of this data shows the payment was not effective as a long term solution.

- Customer success was 92% in the first 30 days. This is close to the projection at this point in time.
- Follow-up data at 60 days reveals that not all of those who achieved 30 days of stability were able to maintain it; 85% remain in their homes after 60 days.
- After 90 days, families increasingly lose their housing; with only 58% remaining in their homes.

ROMA Logic Model 1.0 – Emergency Housing Example

National ROMA Peer-To-Peer Training Program

Organization: CAA **Program: Emergency Housing** ☑ **Family Level**

Need	Service or Activity	Outcome	Projected Indicator	Actual Indicator	Measurement Tool	Data Procedures	Frequency
(1) Planning	(2) Intervention	(3) Benefit	(4) Performance	(5) Performance	(6) Accountability	(7) Accountability	(8) Accountability
	200 families will receive housing assistance, during fiscal year July 1 to June 30			**203 families actually received housing assistance, July 1, - June 30**			
Families are at risk of being evicted.	One month emergency rent payment will be issued for 150 families within the program year.	Families remain in their own residence.	150 of 150, or 100%, of families will remain in their own residence for 30 days.	**142 of 155, or 92%, of families remain in their own residence 30 days.** **132 of 155, or 85%, of families remain in their own residence 60 days.** **90 of 155, or 58%, of families remain in their own residence 90 days**	Housing application Housing activity log showing payments. Record of paying rent Family report during follow up. Copies of current payments.	Case record. Data entered into automated case record at time of encounter. Data entered by CAA case-manager.	Data collected at time of encounter. Summary report generated to supervisor daily. Weekly report generated to department head each Monday. Monthly report generated for executive director.
Families are homeless.	Up to 30 days of emergency shelter services will be provided for 50 families within the program year.	Homeless families reside in safe temporary shelter.	50 of 50, or 100%, of homeless families will reside in safe shelter for up to 30 days.	**48 of 48, or 100%, of homeless families resided in safe shelter for 7 to 30 days.**	Shelter log. Family report during follow up.	Case Record. Data entered into case record at time of encounter. Data entered by shelter case-manager.	Data collected at time of encounter. Daily electronic report emailed to CAA at daily close of business.

Mission: To ensure that all families have safe, clean shelter.

Program Evaluation and Program Improvement

This CAA used the logic model to document the Emergency Housing program results and monitor performance. Collecting and analyzing follow-up outcome and performance data revealed the limits of the intervention of the one month rent payment and suggested that other factors may be adversely affecting families in the community.

The logic model, Housing Assistance 2.0, documents an expanded need resulting from analysis of data in the 1.0 logic model. Because of this analysis, the CAA revised its mission, added interventions, and is now expecting additional outcomes.

These outcomes are characterized with the added dimension of time represented by short-, intermediate-, and long-term.

The agency identified additional funding to provide the newly added interventions to 50 of the customers from its total population of 200. It felt that these customers would come from the emergency rent service. However, this is not identified on the logic model. The agency left this vague so that the additional services could also be available to the customers from emergency shelter, as it did not know who would be interested in the additional services.

Use of this logic model demonstrates a CAA's responsiveness to data analysis and its effectiveness in handling change and obtaining results.

This is Community Action!

ROMA Logic Model 2.0 – Housing Assistance Example

National ROMA Peer-To-Peer Training Program

Organization: CAA Program: Housing Assistance ☑ Family Level

Need	Service or Activity	Outcome	Projected Indicator	Actual Indicator	Measurement Tool	Data Procedures	Frequency
(1) Planning	**(2) Intervention**	**(3) Benefit**	**(4) Performance**	**(5) Performance**	**(6) Accountability**	**(7) Accountability**	**(8) Accountability**
Families are at risk of being evicted.	One month emergency rent payment will be issued for 150 families.	**Short Term** Families remain in their own residence.	**Short Term** 150 of 150, or 100%, of families remain in their own residence 30 days. **Revised to project** 100 out of 150 or 67% of families will remain in their own residence for 90 days.	**Short Term** 142 of 155, or 92%, of families remained in their own residence 30 days. 132 of 155, or 85%, of families remained in their own residence 60 days. 90 of 155, or 58%, of families remained in their own residence 90 days	Housing application (for date of request). Housing activity log showing payments. Record of paying rent Family report during follow up.	Case record. Data entered into automated case record at time of encounter. Data entered by CAA case-manager.	Data collected at time of encounter. Summary report generated to supervisor daily. Weekly report generated to department head each Monday. Monthly report generated for executive director.
Families are homeless.	Up to 30 days of emergency shelter services will be provided for 50 families within the program year.	**Short Term** Homeless families reside in safe temporary shelter.	50 of 50, or 100%, of homeless families will reside in safe shelter for up to 30 days.	48 of 48, or 100%, of homeless families resided in safe shelter for 7 to 30 days.	Shelter log. Family report during follow up.	Case Record. Data entered into case record at time of encountered by shelter case mgr.	Data collected at time of encounter. Daily report emailed to CAA at daily.
	50 families will receive additional housing assistance 7/1 – 6/30			**65 families received additional housing assistance 7/1-6/30**			
Families are unable to maintain housing	Transitional housing will be provided to 30 families for up to 270 days during the program year.	**Intermediate** Families reside in temporary subsidized housing.	**Intermediate Term** 30 of 50, or 60%, of families will reside in transitional housing within the program year:	**Intermediate Term** 32 of 65, or 49%, of families resided in transitional housing for 30 to 270 days within the program year:	Approved Housing Application Transitional Housing records Family report during follow up.	Case record. Data entered into automated case record at time of encounter, by CAA case-manager.	Weekly report to department head each Monday. Monthly report for executive director.
After 90 days, 42% of the families lost their residence.	During the program year Housing Assistance will be provided to 20 families: --Arrangements made for public housing for 15 families, --Arrangements will be made for unsubsidized rental housing for 4 families, --pre-purchase counseling provided to 1 family.	**Long Term** Families obtain permanent housing.	**Long Term** Within program year: 15 of 50 or 30%, of families secure public housing, 4 of 50, or 7%, obtain unsubsidized affordable rental housing, 1 of 50, or 2%, purchased a home.	**Long Term** Within program year: 12 of 65 or 18%, of families secured public housing; 21 of 65, or 32%, obtained unsubsidized affordable rental housing, 0 of 65 purchased a home.	Lease Rent receipts t Family report during follow up. Mortgage. or other closing documents.	City public housing records or **private landlord** reported to CAA case-manager.	Reported to CAA case-manager supervisor monthly, quarterly reports to executive director.

Mission: To ensure that all families have safe, clean shelter and affordable permanent housing.

Relationship of the Logic Model to an Outcome Scale

Do you have this question: "Which comes first, the logic model or the outcome scale?"

The answer is that either one can be created independently.

The logic model, which can be used for planning, may also contain the elements to develop an Outcome Scale. In the logic model we have been working with, there are sufficient elements to construct an Outcome Scale as shown below.

This Housing Outcome Scale was developed using the "Housing Assistance Logic Model" from previous pages.

Outcome Level: ☑ Family **Domain: Housing**

Benchmarks	
Thriving	Secure home ownership (from long-term outcome)
Safe	Maintain unsubsidized affordable rental (from long-term outcome)
Stable	Remain in own residence (from short-term outcome) Public housing (from long-term outcome) Transitional housing (from intermediate-term outcome)
	Prevention Line
Vulnerable	Staying in Emergency Shelter (from short term outcome) At-risk of eviction (from need statement)
In-Crisis	Homeless (from need statement)

Using an Outcome Scale to Help with Setting Targets

An Outcome Scale can be adapted to include data on the progress of a group of participants through a program and can be a useful tool in the process of establishing realistic performance targets for the agency's programs and services.

The following is an adaptation of Logic Model 2.0 to develop an Outcome Scale for collecting and analyzing projected and actual data.

Benchmarks	Housing Outcomes	# Projected	# Actual
Thriving	Secure home ownership	1	0
Safe	Maintain unsubsidized affordable rental	4	21
Stable	Remain in own residence Public housing Transitional housing	100 15 30	90 12 32

Documentation of the program indicates the projected and actual end state for each scale benchmark.

Consider the agency's targeting ability. *Each of the outcomes has a different targeting success rate. What do we learn from this?*

How can this data help the program set targets for next year?

Identify what targets may be changed based on experience.

Analysis of Data

Consider the analysis techniques we suggested to "make meaning" out of your community needs assessment data. Those same techniques can be applied to the data you collect and enter into your agency reporting tools.

- **Aggregate the Data** – Bring discrete data together so it can be analyzed.
- **Count** the number of some element that is important to you.
- **Compare** data elements to begin to see relationships that might increase knowledge about the situation.
- **Look at the trends** that you see. Is there a pattern in the data?

Analysis techniques may uncover unexpected relationships that will provide additional ideas to improve results.

ROMA tools (Carter Questions, Scales, Matrices, Logic Models) can identify data elements to evaluate performance. Data from fiscal, human resources and other parts of the agency should be part of your data analysis. Data collected throughout the ROMA Cycle can be brought together in the Evaluation phase of the cycle. Analysis of data will help you consider what may be needed for the next Community Needs Assessment.

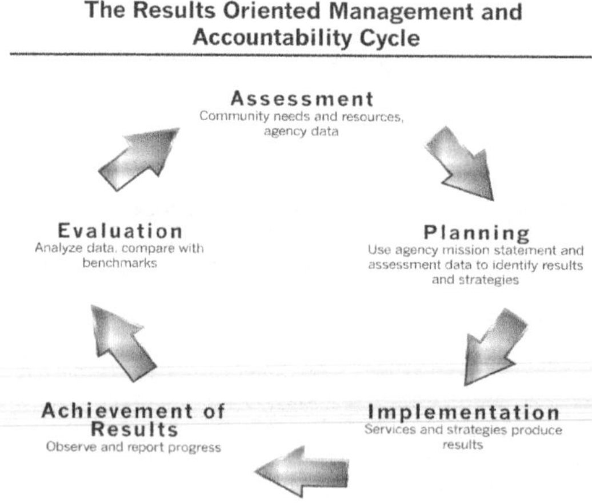

The ROMA Cycle provides you with the structure for continuous quality improvement.

Module Seven Review

1. A logic model is a tool that links program__________ and program __________.

2. A logic model is a good tool for planning, but cannot be used in any other phase of the ROMA Cycle. True or False

3. The ROMA Logic Model is like a story with a connecting narrative, so the data entered in all eight columns must match or be connected to the other columns. True or False

4. A service that is designed to meet an immediate (emergency) need does not have to produce any change in the life of an individual or family. True or False.

5. Once a homeless family is placed in an Emergency Shelter, the agency cannot provide any additional services. True or False

6. A Logic Model may include different outcomes: those that are achieved in the short term, __________ term or ______ term.

7. If you use the ROMA Logic Model, you will never use an Outcome Scale. True or False

8. However you collect data, it must be analyzed to become useful for improving program results. True or False

9. Analysis of data would not reveal unexpected relationships between services and outcomes because those connections are too difficult to discover. True or False

10. The ROMA Cycle provides a structure for continuous quality improvement. True or False

Closing

Key Points

- Recognize the need to devise a plan to help CAAs, State offices, and the CSBG network implement ROMA.
- Acknowledge the use of the Ten Questions as an example of a pre- and post-measure of increased knowledge.

Implementing the ROMA Cycle

Next Steps

- Recognize the nature of the ROMA process and how it affects all aspects of the management of your CAA, future funding and relationships to funders.
- Gain commitment of all stakeholders including the Board, Executive Director, management, and staff for the full implementation of ROMA to include a focus on outcomes and performance in addition to activities or outputs.
- Develop outcomes for specific programs and services using the ROMA Logic Model. Use logic models to develop a common management and reporting framework.
- Develop outcome scales and matrices for programs and services that support and assist the customer through an incremental change process.
- Develop an internal quality assurance process to support your agency's accountability.
- Work towards implementing a common customer identifier and common customer intake system to assure an unduplicated count.
- Recognize the need to gather and report on different data sets for various funders.
- Develop common and acceptable outcome measures useful to multiple funders.
- Identify the information that is needed to support on-going results-oriented management and accountability. Wait to develop your management information system until after you know what information you need.
- Integrate ROMA concepts and language into assessment, planning, reporting, and evaluation processes; and into fiscal and human resources policies and procedures.
- Identify information to be used to convey or market the outcomes or impact of the interventions outside the CAA.
- Train all staff and board members in basic ROMA principles and practices.

Reinventing Organizations*

1. What gets measured gets done.

2. If you do not measure results, you cannot tell success from failure.

3. If you cannot see success, you cannot reward it.

4. If you cannot reward success, you are probably rewarding failure.

5. If you cannot see success, you cannot learn from it.

6. If you cannot recognize failure, you cannot correct it.

7. If you can demonstrate results, you can win public support.

**Reinventing Government*, David Osborne & Ted Gaebler, 1992. Addison-Wesley Publishing Company, Reading, MA 01867, (617) 944-3700 Ext. 2431.

The Ten Questions – Revisited

1. True or False: "ROMA" is the term for the required reporting of data to state and federal government funding sources.

2. True or False: Each phase of the ROMA cycle is most effective when conducted in isolation from other phases.

3. True or False: The ROMA Cycle is completed when reports are compiled and submitted.

4. True or False: Community Action agencies (CAAs) most effectively evaluate their results by focusing on the activities supported exclusively by the Community Services Block Grant (CSBG) which sponsors ROMA.

5. True or False: The 2017 National Theory of Change maintains the historic National Goals, including family, agency and community goals, but is in graphic form.

6. True or False: The focus on results instead of the provision of services will reduce the agency's competitiveness and marketability because of low numbers of results reported.

7. True or False: "Outcomes" and "Services" are different terms for the same concept.

8. True or False: According to the Organizational Standards, when creating the agency plan, CAAs are required to select services they will offer based on funding they have available.

9. True or False: Implementing ROMA in your CAA will affect the planning and fiscal functions, but will not affect the way programs and services are delivered.

10. True or False: ROMA Next Generation is an improved management system because it uses different foundational principles than the original ROMA created in 1994.

Answers: All are False.

Blank Forms

OUTCOME SCALE

ROMA LOGIC MODEL – ONE DIMENSION

ROMA LOGIC MODEL – MULTIPLE DIMENSIONS

BLANK OUTCOME SCALE

Outcome Level ☐ Family ☐ Agency ☐ Community

Benchmarks	
Thriving	
Safe	
Stable	
	Prevention Line
Vulnerable	
In-Crisis	

ROMA Logic Model

National ROMA Peer-To-Peer Training Program

Organization: **Program:** ☐ **Family**

Need **Problem, Situation**	**Intervention** **Service or Activity** Identify the # of customers to be served and the time frame for the project. *May also include the # of units of service offered.*	**Outcome** General statement of results expected without numbers	**Projected Outcome Indicator** # of customers expected to achieve each outcome divided by the number expected to be served; projected % of customer success	**Actual Outcome Indicator** # of customers actually achieving the outcome, divided by the number actually served; actual % of customer success	**Measurement Tools** What evidence will you collect to prove your outputs were delivered and outcomes were achieved?	**Data Procedures** Include Collection, Storage and Analysis Procedure; Personnel Responsible	**Frequency of Data Collection, Reporting and Analysis**
(1) Planning	**(2) Intervention**	**(3) Benefit**	**(4) Performance**	**(5) Performance**	**(6) Accountability**	**(7) Accountability**	**(8) Accountability**
Mission:							

ROMA Logic Model – S, I, L dimensions
National ROMA Peer-To-Peer Training Program

Organization: **Program:** □ **Family**

Need **Problem, Situation**	**Intervention** **Service or Activity** Identify the # of customers to be served and the time frame for the project. *May also include the # of units of service offered.*	**Outcome** General statement of results expected without numbers	**Projected Outcome Indicator** # of customers expected to achieve each outcome divided by the number expected to be served; projected % of customer success	**Actual Outcome Indicator** # of customers actually achieving the outcome, divided by the number actually served; actual % of customer success	**Measurement Tools** What evidence will you collect to prove your outputs were delivered and outcomes were achieved?	**Data Procedures** Include Collection, Storage and Analysis Procedure; Personnel Responsible	**Frequency of Data Collection, Reporting and Analysis**
(1) Planning	**(2) Intervention**	**(3) Benefit**	**(4) Performance**	**(5) Performance**	**(6) Accountability**	**(7) Accountability**	(8) Accountability
		Short Term	**Short Term**	**Short Term**			
		Intermediate Term	**Intermediate Term**	**Intermediate Term**			
		Long Term	**Long Term**	**Long Term**			
Mission:							

NOTES

Made in the USA
Middletown, DE
20 October 2020

22379200R00097